Vanishing Life

Vanishing Life

THE MYSTERY OF MASS EXTINCTIONS

Jeff Hecht

CHARLES SCRIBNER'S SONS · NEW YORK

Maxwell Macmillan Canada · Toronto
Maxwell Macmillan International
New York · Oxford · Singapore · Sydney

Charles Scribner's Sons Books for Young Readers
Macmillan Publishing Company, 866 Third Avenue, New York, NY 10022

Maxwell Macmillan Canada, Inc.
1200 Eglinton Avenue East, Suite 200, Don Mills, Ontario M3C 3N1

Macmillan Publishing Company is part of the Maxwell Communication Group
of Companies.

First edition   10 9 8 7 6 5 4 3 2 1
Printed in the United States of America
Designed by Kathryn Parise

Library of Congress Cataloging-in-Publication Data
Hecht, Jeff.
Vanishing life : the mystery of mass extinctions / Jeff Hecht.—1st ed.
    p.   cm.   Includes bibliographical references (p.   ) and index.
Summary: Explores the phenomenon of mass extinctions of plant and
animal species throughout history.
ISBN 978-1-4169-9422-0   ISBN 1-4169-9422-X
1. Extinction (Biology)—Juvenile literature.   [1. Extinction (Biology)]   I. Title.
QE721.2.E97H43 1993   575'.7—dc20   92-41713

To Leah and Jolyn,
looking forward to their own adventures

Contents

Acknowledgments

Over the years I have been writing for *New Scientist* magazine many scientists have given generously of their time to tell me about their studies of our planet's past and the evolution of life. Their time and research helped make this book possible. I also owe special thanks to the following:

Luis and Walter Alvarez, for getting me interested; Richard Staley, for reviewing a draft version of the book; Chris Scotese, for helping me understand the planet's history and for sharing his maps of the ancient earth; Jody Bourgeois, for taking me to explore real rocks; Sarah Fowell, for reviewing a draft chapter; Dale Russell, for patiently answering my questions on dinosaurs; *New Scientist* magazine, for providing a base for my explorations; To The Point Graphics of Newton, Massachusetts, for artistic skills I lack; and Clare Costello, for deciding this was the best idea.

1

The Ruins of Ancient Empires

Imagine finding the ruins of an ancient empire. The people have long gone, and the buildings have fallen down. Look around, and your mind fills with questions. Who lived there? How long ago? Where did they come from? What did they do? Where did they go? Why did the empire fall?

We must look in many places to solve those mysteries. Legends and old records from other ancient sites may tell of the fallen city. Scientists can find clues by sifting the soil and studying the ruins. They may find old messages written in a forgotten language. They may find relics the ancient people left, from ornaments buried in graves to bits of food from garbage pits. Like detectives they sort through the evidence and piece together pictures of ancient empires, of Egypt and Mesopotamia, of the Maya and the Etruscans.

Empires of a different sort rose and fell long before people built cities or walked the earth. Just 18,000 years ago, before people learned how to farm, thick ice sheets covered Canada and parts of the northern United States, and woolly mammoths and mastodons roamed the frozen tundra of Nebraska. Three million years ago, fierce meat-eating birds ten feet (three meters) tall roamed the Americas. Dinosaurs ruled the earth for 150 million years, along with other giant reptiles that flew and

The vanished underwater empire of sea scorpions about 420 million years ago. Horseshoe crabs are the closest living relatives of these long-extinct animals. Modern insects, spiders, scorpions, crabs, and lobsters are more distant relations. (Courtesy of Field Museum of Natural History, Chicago [Neg. #GEO80819])

lived in the sea. Before the dinosaurs there were other empires, ruled by strange reptiles with sails on their backs, by giant fish with thick armor, or by animals called sea scorpions that could grow as big as a person.

Some of these ancient empires faded away quietly, but others fell mysteriously. The dinosaurs and their kin all died about 65 million years ago. Between 12,000 and 9,000 years ago, the mammoths, mastodons, dire wolves, and most other big Ice Age mammals died out in North America. So many living things became extinct at those times that scientists call them mass extinctions. Any extinction changes the world a little, but a mass extinction changes the world a lot. The mass extinction that claimed the dinosaurs divides two geologic eras, the Mesozoic (meaning "middle life") and the Cenozoic (meaning "recent life"). The worst mass extinction occurred 245 million years ago, dividing the Paleozoic era of ancient life from the Mesozoic.

Like many other people, I had passed by the ruins of these ancient empires many times before something caught my eye. It was an article in *Science* magazine, which said that a global disaster might have killed the dinosaurs. I was supposed to be looking for articles on lasers, but this one was much more interesting. Curious, I started reading more about extinctions and the history of the earth. The more I learned, the more interested I grew. I talked with scientists, attended meetings, and wrote articles for magazines. I became caught up in the mystery of mass extinctions, looking for patterns. I've been watching for a dozen years as scientists have found some answers, and many more mysteries. There is plenty more to explore.

Extinctions and Life

Some extinctions are puzzles from the past, but others continue today. People have seen many types of plants and animals, called species, die or come close to extinction. Some species were rare, or like the dodo, lived only in one place. Others, like the passenger pigeon, were once common. A few, like the whooping crane and the American bison (the buffalo of the Wild West), became very rare but are recovering. Some extinctions are a natural part of the way the world changes, with new plants and animals replacing old ones. However, humans caused most recent extinctions, including that of the dodo and passenger pigeon, and almost wiped out the bison and whooping crane. Some scientists even say we are in the midst of another mass extinction, for which we can only blame ourselves.

The possible reasons for past mass extinctions have been debated for many years. Some scientists believe the world changed so much that older plants and animals could not survive. The climate may have grown too hot or too cold, or the seas may have risen or fallen. Others blame new predators, new grazing animals, or even new plants that older animals could not digest. Still others think great disasters may have killed vast numbers of living things.

There is a difference between death and extinction. Individual animals die. People kill millions of mice, but many million more survive, so the species remains alive. A species goes extinct when the last individual dies. The smaller the numbers of any plant or animal, the easier it is for it to go extinct. The rhinoceros is endangered because only about eleven thousand rhinos survive in the entire world. The California condor is severely endangered because only a few dozen survive. A species may become extinct if a disaster kills all the individuals, or if its numbers drop slowly for natural reasons.

We know that mass extinctions have changed the world. The deaths of old species make room for new ones. If the dinosaurs had survived, they would have left little room for the mammals that evolved into people. Some scientists think that extinctions may have shaped the course of life on Earth. We humans may be changing the course of life today, as we clear tropical forests, cause extinctions, and occupy more and more land. This environmental connection adds extra importance to the mystery of mass extinctions.

What Killed the Dinosaurs?

Dinosaurs are the superstars of the past. The first living cells date back at least 3.5 billion years. Fossils of complex animals date back more than half a billion years. Countless animals have lived and died since then, but none have gotten as much attention as the dinosaurs.

People have known for hundreds of years that rocks contained bones of long-dead animals. However, only in the nineteenth century did scientists put together the fossil bones to make the skeletons of giant reptiles they called dinosaurs, from the Greek word for "fearful lizards." It was a time when people were fascinated by the strange and exotic.

Americans flocked to see Jumbo the elephant in Phineas T. Barnum's traveling circus; they had never seen such a huge creature. The fossils showed that dinosaurs had been even larger, and like Jumbo, their size and strangeness made them stars.

Like circus owners, nineteenth-century scientists searched the globe for more and more unusual creatures. Two of these scientists, Edward D. Cope and Othniel Charles Marsh, were Americans who had money to spend, were fascinated by dinosaurs—and were archrivals. Each wanted to find better fossils than the other. They heard of rich fossil deposits in the western United States, so they sent fossil hunters searching the Wild West for ancient bones. Men like Charles Sternberg dodged outlaws and hostile Indians and found spectacular fossils, which they sent east to museums.

As scientists found more dinosaur fossils, they began to see how the animals changed with time. Dinosaurs had developed from smaller reptiles. The dinosaurs themselves evolved over many millions of years. Brontosaurus and stegosaurus lived long before tyrannosaurus and triceratops. Younger rocks contained no dinosaur fossils at all. Mammals, which had been tiny in the dinosaur age, began growing larger.

At first it was not clear what had happened. Very few plants and animals leave fossils, and very little of the past is preserved. Some scientists thought they simply had not found the right rocks to show how large mammals conquered the dinosaurs. Now we know that no such rocks ever existed. The dinosaurs, the giant marine reptiles, the flying pterosaurs, and many other animals died out about 65 million years ago, when mammals were not much larger than rats. Bigger mammals evolved only after the dinosaurs were gone. The mystery deepened.

What happened to the dinosaurs? People today may call old and bulky things "dinosaurs," but in fact dinosaurs were very successful animals. They dominated the land for 150 million years, much longer than mammals—and more than a thousand times longer than modern humans have lived. Yet something went wrong, and they became extinct.

The dinosaurs were not alone. Many other animals died at the same time, in one of the largest mass extinctions in the history of the earth.

Yet we think of the dinosaurs first because they were the most famous, like a singer or a senator killed in a plane crash. To try to solve the mystery of mass extinctions, we must look at all the victims and compare them to the plants and animals that did survive. As we will see later, that pattern and other evidence point to a tremendous disaster that devastated the entire planet.

Other Mass Extinctions

However, one disaster that killed the dinosaurs is not the whole story. There were several other points in the earth's history when many animals went extinct at about the same time. (Table 1 lists the times and the victims.)

One of the earliest mass extinctions happened more than half a billion years ago. Its main victims were trilobites, small animals like insects that lived in the ocean until about 245 million years ago. They may not sound important now, but 500 million years ago trilobites dominated the seas, and very little lived on the land. Rocks formed at the time show the change, although scientists had to look carefully to find it. Paleontologist Rob Thomas showed them to me in the House Range of Utah. Many types of trilobite fossils lie below the layer that marks the mass extinction, but few lie right above it. Something killed the trilobites.

The worst mass extinction was not the one that got the dinosaurs but the one that—in a sense—cleared the planet for them. On land it wiped out many early reptiles, leaving those that would evolve into dinosaurs. It did much more damage to ocean life. It killed up to 96 percent of the species of hard-shelled animals that leave most fossils found on ancient ocean floors. It made so many changes that geologists call the event the end of the Paleozoic era of old life. The reptiles that survived on land evolved into many different groups, including dinosaurs, turtles, crocodiles, pterosaurs, marine reptiles, lizards, and snakes. One group of reptiles evolved into mammals, about the same time the first dinosaurs appeared.

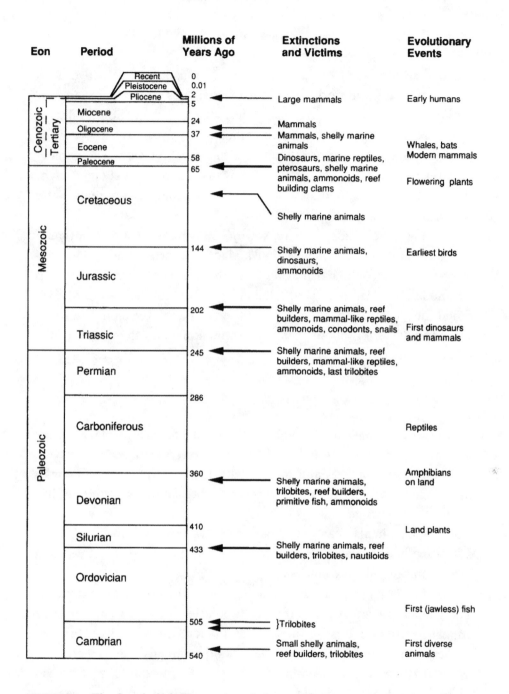

Eon	Period	Millions of Years Ago	Extinctions and Victims	Evolutionary Events
	Recent	0		
	Pleistocene	0.01		
	Pliocene	2	Large mammals	Early humans
		5		
Cenozoic / Tertiary	Miocene	24	Mammals	
	Oligocene	37	Mammals, shelly marine animals	Whales, bats
	Eocene			Modern mammals
	Paleocene	58	Dinosaurs, marine reptiles, pterosaurs, shelly marine animals, ammonoids, reef building clams	
		65		Flowering plants
Mesozoic	Cretaceous		Shelly marine animals	
		144	Shelly marine animals, dinosaurs, ammonoids	Earliest birds
	Jurassic			
		202	Shelly marine animals, reef builders, mammal-like reptiles, ammonoids, conodonts, snails	First dinosaurs and mammals
	Triassic	245	Shelly marine animals, reef builders, mammal-like reptiles, ammonoids, last trilobites	
Paleozoic	Permian	286		
	Carboniferous			Reptiles
		360	Shelly marine animals, trilobites, reef builders, primitive fish, ammonoids	Amphibians on land
	Devonian	410		Land plants
	Silurian	433	Shelly marine animals, reef builders, trilobites, nautiloids	
	Ordovician			First (jawless) fish
		505	}Trilobites	
	Cambrian	540	Small shelly animals, reef builders, trilobites	First diverse animals

TABLE 1 *The last half billion years of the earth's history, showing geologic periods, evolutionary events, and mass extinctions. Darker arrows indicate the largest extinctions.*

Scientists look for patterns in mass extinctions just as detectives look for patterns in similar crimes. However, the clues scientists have found show that each mass extinction is somewhat different. Some affected many types of plants and animals; others only a few. Whatever killed the dinosaurs did little harm to animals in the deep ocean. The number of extinctions also varies widely; some mass extinctions claimed many victims, others so few that some scientists wonder if they really were *mass* extinctions.

We may be coming close to solving one mass-extinction mystery. Scientists have good evidence that a giant meteorite 6 miles (10 kilometers) across hit the earth at the time the dinosaurs died. One clue is a buried crater 110 miles (180 kilometers) across, in the part of Mexico called the Yucatán, that seems to be the right age. Yet many questions remain unanswered about that mass extinction—and the causes of the others are less well known.

Extinctions and Evolution

Extinctions are part of the complex story of life on our planet. Over millons of years, plants and animals have slowly changed, or evolved, to fit their environment and to deal with the other plants and animals that share the world. Mass extinctions have helped shape evolution, like a forest fire changes the woods. On one hand, extinction wipes out plants and animals that might have evolved into new forms. On the other, extinction leaves the world open for survivors, like trees that sprout on burned-over land.

We owe our place in the world to the mass extinction of the dinosaurs. The giant reptiles had captured all the places the world had for large animals; mammals about the size of modern rodents lived in their shadow. Only after the dinosaurs died could mammals grow larger. With the world to themselves, mammals (and birds) evolved in many different ways. Some, from bison and elephants to rabbits and beavers, became plant eaters. Others, like wolves, bears, and lions, became meat eaters.

A few evolved into human beings. They would not have had the chance had the dinosaurs survived.

Extinction is a loss, but it is also part of the natural cycle of life and evolution. Life is always changing; new species appear and old ones die. The average species of plant or animal lives about four million years— a long time in human terms, but a short time compared to the 4.5-billion-year age of the earth. We sometimes forget this when we look at the past. We may think that the same dinosaurs lived through the whole Age of Reptiles. Yet brontosaurus and stegosaurus lived tens of millions of years before triceratops and the duck-billed dinosaurs.

To see the difference between mass extinctions and the natural slow change of life, think of a forest. Trees of all ages live in a natural forest. Some are young saplings, but a few are dead or dying of old age or disease. Those few dead trees are like the victims of natural extinctions. A mass extinction is something that fells all the trees in the forest—a fire, a tornado, or a logging crew making a clear-cut.

Look carefully at the remains, and you can tell what happened to a fallen forest. Blackened soil and charred stumps tell you the forest burned. Tree trunks broken and scattered like matchsticks tell you a tornado tore the forest apart. Neatly sawed stumps and piles of branches tell you that people cut down the trees.

The causes of mass extinction of animals are much harder to identify. We must learn to read the language of the rocks, which tell the tales of the past. We must learn about the history of life and how it evolved. We must learn how scientific detectives put the pieces of evidence together—and often disagree about what the evidence means. Only after we lay that groundwork can we grapple with the mystery of mass extinction itself.

Be warned that this real-life mystery lacks the neat solutions to be found at the end of detective stories. Scientists have a good idea what may have got the dinosaurs, but they aren't certain. They have some guesses about other mass extinctions of the past, but they don't know if any of their guesses are right. Lots of work is left to do to solve the mystery of mass extinctions—and that will make it fun for scientists for many years to come.

Extinctions also connect with the environment. Like the loggers who clear-cut the forest, human beings are causing a new wave of extinctions. Many scientists believe that the first Americans caused the extinctions of giant mammals ten thousand to twelve thousand years ago. Modern clearing of tropical forests is wiping out about thirty-three species a day. We may be causing a mass extinction that could change the face of the planet as surely as did the death of the dinosaurs.

2

Reading the Rocks

W̶e know human history from words and pictures that people have written. We know the earth's history from what nature has written in rocks. The rocks do not record every detail, any more than history books list each meal that people ate. Some pages of the earth's history have been lost. But rocks are where we must turn to find the evidence of past events and to solve the mystery of mass extinctions.

Some clues to the past are easy to see, like big dinosaur bones. Others are easy to miss unless you know them, like the tiny footprints of animals that lived on the ocean floor. Some are too tiny to see without a magnifying glass or microscope, like the fossils of pollen and microbes. Some are parts of the rocks themselves, and the minerals they contain.

Geologists learn how to read rocks like other people learn how to read foreign languages. Different rocks have different languages, and no geologist reads all of them. Some read fossil pollen, to learn about plants and the conditions where they grew. Others read the layering of the rocks, to tell when and how they formed. Some study how the continents have changed; others look at fossil plants or animals.

These clues can tell us about extinctions and other changes in life. To understand them, we need to learn some history of our planet. It is background we need to solve the extinction mystery—like detectives need to know the backgrounds of victims, what they did, and how they lived.

The Story of the Earth

Scientists believe the solar system formed 4.5 billion years ago from a cloud of gas and dust. Most material went into the sun; some formed the planets. A little bit was left over, and it formed smaller chunks of ice and rock. Blocks of rocky ice are called comets; as they come close to the sun, some ice evaporates, giving them bright halos and tails. Most

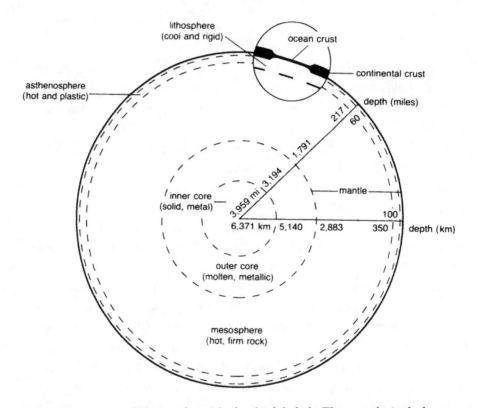

Internal structure of the earth, with depths labeled. The mantle includes two layers of molten rock—the hot, soft asthenosphere and the firmer but also hot mesosphere—as well as the lower part of the lithosphere.

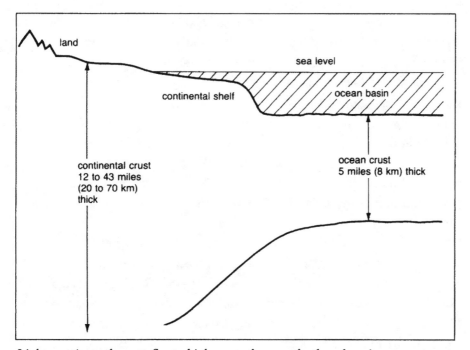

Light continental crust floats higher on the mantle than heavier ocean crust. Water fills the low ocean basins and covers the outer fringes of the continents, called the continental shelf.

comets are beyond the orbits of Neptune and Pluto, but a few are much closer to the sun. The chunks of rock are called asteroids, which mostly orbit between Mars and Jupiter. Some small rocks, dust, and gas also orbit the sun, but it's the asteroids and comets that are important in the extinction mystery.

The young Earth was hot and molten. Gravity pulled the heaviest materials, iron and other metals, down to form the core of the planet. Heavy molten rocks surrounded the core, forming a layer called the mantle. Lighter liquid rock floated to the surface, where it cooled enough to form a thin, solid crust. The crust has grown thicker, but energy from the decay of radioactive elements keeps the center of the earth hot.

Heat energy still leaks from deep in the earth. That heat makes the mantle and even the solid crust move, like water warming in a pan, but very, very much more slowly. The earth's crust moves an inch or two (a few centimeters) a year—about as fast as your toenails grow. That does not sound like much, but it builds up huge force over many years and causes great earthquakes.

This slow motion has formed two kinds of crust on the surface: continental and ocean crust. Lighter rock makes up the continents, which are 12 to 43 miles (20 to 70 kilometers) thick and seem to float on the mantle. Denser ocean crust, about 5 miles (8 kilometers) thick, floats lower on the mantle, forming the low areas on the earth's surface. The earth has more than enough water to fill the ocean basins, so shallow seas cover the low edges of the continents, called continental shelves.

The continents and ocean floors are broken into large chunks called plates, which move on the surface in what geologists call plate tectonics. The motion is very slow, but in millions of years it changes the map. The South Atlantic Ocean grew after Africa and South America ripped apart 100 to 130 million years ago.

Light continental rocks float on the surface, but heavier ocean crust can sink into the mantle, at places called subduction trenches. The oldest parts of continents are about four billion years old; the oldest ocean floor is under 200 million years old. As old ocean crust sinks, new ocean crust forms at "spreading centers," where the old crust is pulled apart and molten rock rises to the surface. It's a little like something cooking on a stove, but very, very, very much slower.

How Rocks Form

Rocks on the earth's surface have varied origins. Some, called *igneous* rocks, formed when molten rock cooled and became solid. They came in two types. *Volcanic* rocks form when lava erupts and cools on the surface on land or under the sea; basalt is an example. *Plutonic* rocks form when the molten rock freezes solid without ever reaching the surface; granite is an example.

Rocks can form in other ways. *Sedimentary* rocks form when material collects in low places, such as valleys, lakes, streambeds, and oceans. The sediments that make them up include everything that wind and water can collect—sand grains, pebbles, dirt, tiny pieces of leaves and wood, old seashells, broken bones of dead animals, dust, and pollen grains. As more sediment piles up, the material on the bottom is pressed into solid rock, like sandstone or shale.

Metamorphic rocks began as sedimentary or igneous rocks. Then they were buried deep underground, where heat and pressure converted them into new types of rock, as if they were cooked. Gneiss and schist are metamorphic rocks.

Each type of rock can tell different stories. Igneous rocks tell how continents grew and moved, but they say little about living things or mass extinctions. When these rocks become solid, any magnetic materials inside them record the earth's magnetic field like tiny fossil compasses that point in the direction that was north when and where they formed. The crystal sizes tell how fast the rocks cooled—the slower the cooling, the larger the crystals.

Only sedimentary rocks contain fossils and other clues about living things. They also contain many other things that give us clues about climate, temperature, and other conditions when the rocks formed. They contain the most valuable clues to mass extinctions, like tiny pieces of rock shattered by a giant meteor impact, or rare elements from the meteor itself.

Metamorphic rocks are like notebooks that went through the washing machine. The pages have stuck together and the ink has run; we can no longer read most of the words, but a few notes written in pencil might survive.

The Geologic Time Scale

The layers of rock record geologic time. The oldest rocks are on the bottom, with younger rocks stacked on top of them. You can see the layering clearly in places like the Grand Canyon. Sediments piled up over millions of years in areas that were low at the time. As local conditions changed, the rocks' colors and textures changed, forming the varied layers we see today. Look closely and you can see some layers are made of even thinner layers, which can be peeled apart almost like the pages of a book. Geologists use this layering to date rocks, but it often isn't easy.

The problem is that the rock layers are like a very messy closet. Someone has added newspapers and magazines each day, so the oldest should be on the bottom. However, some piles have fallen over—rocks pushed around when continents collided. Things were piled in the easiest places to reach at different times—just as nature forms sedimentary rocks in the lowest places. From time to time, someone else has taken some things out of the closet without telling you what—as wind and water wash away some rocks. All this makes it hard to read the ages of rocks exactly.

The dates on old newspapers and magazines can help you organize an old pile of papers. Nature did not write dates on the rocks, so geologists give names to the periods when different rocks formed, without knowing the rocks' actual dates. Those period names are shown in Table 1 on page 7, along with the times in millions of years. It might seem simpler just to use the dates, but it is very hard to get the numbers accurate. (Geologists defined a standard time scale in 1983, but new research keeps giving better dates. That's why you may see different ages in other books. Most of the changes are small—only a few million years—except for the Cambrian period, which started about thirty million years later than geologists had thought.)

Early geologists estimated ages from how fast sediments were deposited and how much flatter they became when they turned into rock. If you added one centimeter of paper to a pile each week, for example, you would estimate a 100-centimeter pile to be two years (100 weeks) old. Geologists' estimates were not exact, but they showed that the earth was many millions of years old, much older than the thousands of years people had thought before.

Rocks don't form that neatly. Sediments pile up at different rates in different places. Very little material drops to the bottom in the middle of a deep ocean, so only .4 inch (1 centimeter) of sediment may collect in a thousand years. Just 2 inches (5 centimeters) would span the time from the Egyptian pyramids to the space age. Yet the Mississippi River can deposit 3 feet (1 meter) of sand near its mouth in a year. A single hurricane or tsunami (tidal wave) can form thicker layers.

Rocks also form at different times in different places. Sediments collect in shallow seas, but the rocks wear down if the land is pushed above the water line. Meanwhile, rocks start forming in another area that had been worn down earlier. New England has been eroding for most of the past 300 million years, since it was crumpled up into tall mountains by a huge continental collision. It has few younger rocks, except for igneous rocks formed when North America later tore away from Africa. While New England eroded, rocks were forming in the southwestern United States, which was largely submerged until about 65 million years ago. No single place on earth has rocks that tell all of the planet's history.

To read all the earth's history, geologists must match similar rocks from many different places. The best way is to look for fossils of species that only lived a short time; rocks that contain them must have been formed about that same time. *Stratigraphy* is the science of using these fossils to catalog when rocks formed and estimate their ages. Stratigraphers usually study very small fossils like teeth and the shells of microscopic animals, which are much more common and changed faster than larger fossils.

Dating Rocks

The layering of rocks tells us the sequence of events, but not their dates. Geologists are content to know the name of a period when rocks formed. They even break periods down into smaller chunks of time. However, period names like Cambrian, Cretaceous, and Eocene don't tell us how many years old the rocks are. Geologists date rocks in a different way, by studying certain atoms in the rocks.

Most atoms are stable and unchanging, but the nuclei of these radioactive atoms are not stable. Seconds, minutes, days, or millions of years after they form, they release energy and change into other nuclei. Each unstable nucleus has a different average lifetime, measured as the *half-life,* which is how long it takes half the atoms to decay. This can serve as a geological clock because all rocks contain a few unstable atoms. As time passes, they decay into other atoms, which stay trapped in the rock. To measure the age of a rock, geologists count how many radioactive atoms it contains and compare that to the number of atoms produced by the decay.

A common geological clock is the decay of a radioactive isotope of the element potassium into the rare gas argon. Another is the decay of uranium atoms into lead. Radioactive clocks work only for igneous rocks, formed by the cooling of molten rock, but they are the best way to date rocks. They sometimes bring surprises, and scientists are still revising the dates assigned to the standard periods.

Understanding Geologic Time

Dating gets less accurate the further back we go in time. Erosion and the slow motion of the plates of the earth's surface have destroyed some older rocks, changed others beyond recognition, and buried some too deep to study. The older the rocks, the less common they are. This means that we know less about the more distant past, something that shows in the geologic time scale. The recent past is divided into much smaller pieces than the distant past. Geologists used to lump the whole first four billion years of the earth's history into a single period called the Precambrian, meaning the time before hard shells evolved and fossils became common in the Cambrian period that followed. Geologists have learned enough to divide the Precambrian into the Archean and Proterozoic, but fossils remain rare and much of that time is little known.

The numbers on the geological time scale remind us that the earth has been around a very long time. The numbers are so large that they may not mean much in human terms. Very few people live more than 100 years. Recorded history dates back about 5,000 years, to ancient

Egypt and Mesopotamia, when people first developed writing. The first modern human beings lived about 100 thousand to 150 thousand years ago. The oldest fossils of human-like creatures date from a few million years ago.

That means we are newcomers. Dinosaurs existed for 165 million years, although they were rare for the first several million years. That is 33,000 times longer than recorded human history. The 65 million years since the extinction of the dinosaurs is 13,000 times the time between the pyramids and the space age. If that 65 million years was a day, the first human-like creatures would have appeared only in the last hour. Modern humans would have evolved in the last few minutes. Recorded history would span only the last seven seconds. A human life span would be only one-tenth of a second.

The shortest intervals measured by ticks of the geological clock are also long on a human scale. Geologists can find signs of a few rapid events, like the tumbled rocks left by a tsunami. However, they usually measure time only in thousands of years. Trying to use the geological clock to look at shorter times is like trying to time a footrace with a calendar. Geologists can't tell if mass extinctions took an hour or five hundred years!

The Changing Map

Motion of the plates on the earth's surface changes the map very slowly. The typical speed of 2 inches (5 centimeters) a year moves a continent only about 13 feet (4 meters) in an eighty-year human lifetime. We can see that only at the borders of plates. The famous San Andreas Fault is the border where the Pacific Plate (which includes some of California) moves north along the North American Plate. Earthquakes can rip apart roads or fences that cross the fault.

It takes millions of years to change the map. After 10 million years, a movement of 2 inches a year amounts to 300 miles (500 kilometers)— the distance across the Mediterranean Sea from Rome to Tunis. After 100 million years, that motion would carry a continent across the 3,000-

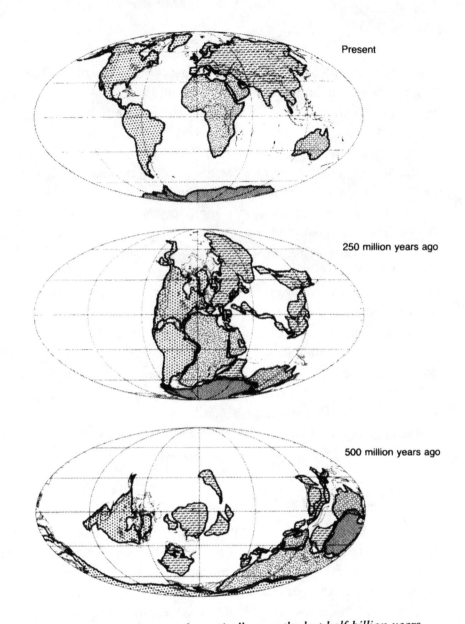

Present

250 million years ago

500 million years ago

Plate motion has changed the map dramatically over the last half billion years. These maps compare the earth 500 and 250 million years ago with the present world, showing how pieces of the continents have moved about the surface. The worst extinction of all time happened about the time of the middle map, when the continents formed a single land mass called Pangaea. (Courtesy of Christopher R. Scotese, University of Texas, Arlington) mile (5,000-kilometer) width of the Atlantic Ocean. That motion has shuffled the map over the last half-billion years, and it will continue. In 50 million years, Los Angeles, west of the San Andreas Fault, will move as far north as Oakland, which lies east of the fault.

Other things change the map faster in different ways. Sea level rises and falls over time. One reason for this is that plate motions change the sizes of the ocean basins, so they hold more or less water. Another reason is the growth and shrinkage of ice caps, which take water from the ocean. At the peak of the last ice age, 18,000 years ago, ice covered most of northern North America and Europe. Sea level then was about 330 feet (100 meters) lower than today, and animals and people could walk across land from Siberia to Alaska. Melting all the ice that remains on Greenland and Antarctica today would raise sea level another 200 feet (60 meters), drowning southern Florida and many other areas.

Changes in the map are clues to mass extinctions. A big rise or fall in sea level could kill the many animals that live on the floors of shallow seas. The coming or going of an ice sheet changes climate dramatically. And over hundreds of millions of years, the continents can move from the poles to the tropics. Half a billion years ago, Florida lay almost at the South Pole, part of a vast southern continent, while the equator ran through Antarctica and the Canadian Arctic. These clues help us understand what fossils have to tell us about the evolution of life on Earth.

3

Fossils: Evidence of
Life and Death

It is a rare thrill to find a fossil, however small it is. My first fossil, about the size of a quarter, was an impression of an insect with its wings spread out. It had fallen into the waters of a shallow tidal flat in the early Triassic, about 240 million years ago. Thin layers of fine silt had covered its body, making a mold that lay buried while the dinosaurs came and went. At last the weather had broken the rock from a canyon wall in Utah, leaving it where I found it on a cool March day. I might not have noticed a living insect, but this fossil from a quarter billion years ago showed me the excitement of searching the past.

Fossils are traces of living things preserved in rocks after they died. While rocks tell us about the history of the earth, fossils tell us about the history of life. We must look at the rocks and fossils together to understand the patterns and mysteries of the past. Fossils are fingerprints of vanished life, and like skeletons found in a ruined city, they can tell us about the ancient empires of life. Fossils can be the most important clues to mass extinctions, but fossil evidence is rare, and its meaning is often unclear. Understanding fossils is a big step toward solving the mystery of mass extinctions.

Nature's Leftovers

Fossils are rare because nature normally recycles the remains of dead plants and animals. Old leaves and dead trees rot and decay; even the wood in our houses will rot if not protected. Insects and other animals eat the remains of dead animals; what is left decays. Even skeletons usually crumble into dust. Nature reuses *almost* everything.

Fossils are nature's leftovers, the parts of living things not recycled into other living things. Some fossils are parts that nothing can eat, like the shells of clams or the teeth of cattle. Other fossils are buried in places where they cannot be recycled, like in a wet peat bog or under a mud slide on the ocean floor. Many fossils are only traces of living things, like dinosaur footprints on a muddy lakeshore, or my impression of an insect.

Most leftovers don't survive. Footprints survive only if something covers them before rain or tides wash them away. Skeletons and shells also survive only if they are protected. A mouse skeleton will erode away faster than an elephant skeleton, but both vanish in time unless they are buried in the right place. Waves break unburied shells into tiny pieces that become part of the sand.

Fossils form only where wind and water pile up sediment to make rocks. Fossils are most likely to survive underwater, in shallow seas, in lakes, or along rivers. Sediments collect in only a few places on land: at the base of tall mountains, in some valleys, and where rivers flow slowly across plains, like the Mississippi River Delta in Louisiana.

Even bones buried in the right place may not survive. They must be buried deep enough to be preserved, but not so deep that the heat and pressure destroys them. If a region rises, erosion can wash away the rocks and bones; this is happening now along the southern California coast. Colliding continents can crush and cook sedimentary rocks, destroying any fossils they contain.

Finally, someone must find the fossils, which isn't easy. Scientists can't go digging up the whole landscape looking for fossils. They have to look where rocks are exposed, like along canyons, streambeds or highways.

They have to come at the right time, after erosion has exposed a fossil, but before the fossil wears away. And they have to notice the fossil and recognize what it is, which takes luck and training.

To see how few animals leave fossils, think about dinosaurs, which were common for over 150 million years. If half a billion dinosaurs of all sizes were alive at any one time, and each lived an average of twenty-five years, that means that 3 million billion dinosaurs—3 quadrillion, or 3,000,000,000,000,000—lived during the dinosaur age. That number is only a rough guess—we don't know how many dinosaurs lived at once or how long they lived—but it shows that there were *lots* of dinosaurs. Now divide that by 2,000—roughly the number of good fossil specimens scientists have found in over one hundred years of searching, not counting loose teeth or small fragments. The result: We have found less than one good fossil for every trillion dinosaurs that ever lived, and only one for every 75 thousand years of the dinosaur era. In short we have missed a lot of the story of life on land.

The origin of birds is an example. About 150 million years ago, an animal called archaeopteryx lived near a shallow sea covering what is now Europe. About the size of a crow, it had wings and feathers like a bird, but teeth and a long tail like a dinosaur. We know about its feathers only because the fine-grained rocks that formed on the ocean bottom preserved vivid imprints of the feathers. Without those imprints, it would have looked like another small dinosaur. Scientists have found five archaeopteryx fossils—but they have not found any feathered ancestors, or any other bird-like animals that lived in the following 15 million years. We know about this link between dinosaurs and birds only because archaeopteryx died in the right place to leave fossils with feathers.

Bony Fossils

Most people think of fossils as bones, and bones can tell much about how animals looked and lived. The huge bones of a brontosaurus tell us it was a giant with a long neck, small head, thick legs, and long tail. The blunt teeth of a hadrosaur show that it ate soft plants; the long

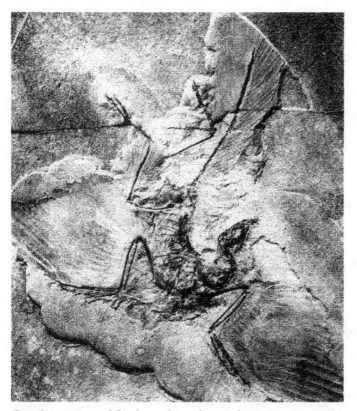

Fossil imprints of feathers show that archaeopteryx was the first bird; without the feathers, it would look like a small dinosaur. (Courtesy of Smithsonian Institution, National Museum of Natural History)

sharp teeth of tyrannosaurus show that it ate meat. Well-preserved bones even show where muscles were attached, giving clues about how dinosaurs walked and ran and what their bodies looked like. Comparing skeletons can show how animals were related.

However, bones don't tell everything. With only bones, we would think archaeopteryx was a small dinosaur. Bones do not tell us when mammals first grew fur, or when they started giving birth to live young. And there are many things bones cannot tell us about how animals lived.

Like many other clues, bones have to be read carefully. The most common fossil bones come from big dinosaurs, but that does not mean the biggest dinosaurs were the most common ones. The bigger bones were just more likely to be fossilized. Some 20 percent of the fossils from the famous Morrison formation came from camarasaurus, a massive 68,000-pound (31,000-kilogram) plant eater. However, Canadian paleontologist Dale Russell says the most common dinosaur living in the region was nanosaurus, a 1.7-pound (.75-kilogram) plant eater, whose small bones were much less likely to be fossilized. In fact, mammals the size of mice or rats may have been more common than any dinosaurs, but they probably spent most of their lives in hiding, and left few fossils other than their tiny teeth.

The Shelly Deep

We are vertebrates, animals with internal bones, so it is only natural that the first fossils we think of are bones. However, the most common fossils are not bones, but the hard shells that protect ocean animals both from currents and from being eaten by other animals. Clam and mussel shells stay on the beach long after the animals that lived in them died. Many other animals also leave shells behind.

Some animals stay in one place on the ocean floor. Some small ones, such as corals, grow shells around themselves. Some live alone, but many live in colonies, which grow their shells on the shells of other animals. Slowly, the hard shells of many generations build up to form massive reefs. Only the outer part is alive; the rest is made of virtually solid fossils. Vast reefs exist in the shallow waters around Australia and the Bahamas. Reefs near southern Florida formed the low, flat islands we call the Florida Keys. Various animals have been building reefs for over half a billion years, leaving thick layers of rock.

Moving animals also left shells on the ocean floor that became fossils. The oldest common fossils are the shells of small animals called trilobites, because their bodies are divided into three "lobes." Distant relatives of insects and horseshoe crabs, they lived from about 530 to 250 million years ago. Like their modern relatives, trilobites shed their hard outer shells as they outgrew them. Each trilobite left an old shell on the ocean floor each time it molted, making plenty of fossils.

Very few creatures eat the shells of ocean animals. As time passes, old shells form thick layers on the ocean floor, like the shells left after a clambake. Most shells are broken or crushed by the weight of the layers on top of them. Eventually large and small shells, reefs, and shell fragments combine to form a type of rock called limestone. Some limestone contains fossils large enough to recognize; other limestone contains only microscopic fragments.

Unusual Fossils

The Petrified Forest National Park in Arizona is famous for a different kind of fossil, logs that have turned into stone. You can find petrified wood in other places too. The ancient wood turned to stone when it was soaked in mineral-rich water. The minerals replaced the soft parts of the wood, but left some harder structures and the shapes of the logs. Petrified wood is harder than the rocks that surround it, so it is left on the ground as the other rocks erode away. Some petrified wood still preserves the original internal structures, letting scientists study ancient trees. A similar process fossilized the oldest land plants, rootless, leafless stems about 2 inches (5 centimeters) tall, which grew about 420 million years ago.

Fossils of soft-bodied animals are extremely rare, but very important to scientists. Normally animals with no hard parts leave no traces behind. However, their bodies sometimes are trapped where they cannot decay, leaving fossils that tell us about these creatures. Some very important fossils were formed over half a billion years ago when mud slid down an underwater slope and buried animals living on the ocean bottom in what is now British Columbia. Nothing disturbed those fossils until geologist Charles Wolcott stumbled upon the rocks he called the Burgess Shale a century ago. Scientists since have found treasure troves of similar fossils in China and Greenland, showing us long-vanished animals that lived at the same time as the trilobites.

Pieces of petrified wood lay exposed on the ground after the soft rock that contained them for over 200 million years eroded away.

Trace Fossils

Bones and shells are not all that animals leave behind. Like people, they leave footprints if they walk through mud. Most footprints are quickly washed away by the next rain or obscured by the tracks of other animals. However, once in a while nature preserves footprints in a sort of natural concrete. Other sediment may cover the mud, burying it and protecting it until it turns to rock. A volcano may scatter fine particles over the mud, which harden to rock and form casts of the footprints.

Dinosaur footprints are the most famous trace fossils. Scientists have matched some footprints with the dinosaurs that made them. Other prints are the only evidence we have of animals that have been extinct for tens of millions of years. Many museums show dinosaur footprints (or, often, casts made from the originals).

A famous set of dinosaur footprints, found in Glen Rose, Texas, by R. T. Bird.
(Courtesy Department Library Services, American Museum of Natural History [Neg.
No. 324393])

Scientists have found many other trace fossils, some hard to recognize. Just as big dinosaur footprints could be preseved on the shore or a streambed, so small footprints of trilobites and other creatures could be preserved on the ocean floor. Nature also preserved a few burrows of worms living in the sea-bottom mud. We don't know what animals made many trace fossils; they are among the mysteries of the past. In the basement of the Pratt Museum at Amherst College I saw one set of tracks that looks like tire prints—in rock more than 500 million years old!

Microfossils and Dating

The most common fossils are the least obvious. They are the tiny hard shells or skeletons of single-celled plants and animals that float in the ocean. Foraminifera are single-celled animals with internal skeletons. Diatoms are single-celled plants with hard shells. These hard parts eventually drift to the bottom of the ocean where they become part of the rocks. They are so small that they are visible only through a microscope.

These tiny shells are important because they can serve as calendars. Each tiny plant or animal had its own shape and lived for a limited time. Scientists have catalogued when these tiny plants and animals lived. By matching the types found in a rock, they can tell when the rock formed. The idea is the same as finding the age of an old newspaper by looking at the names in a baseball box score and finding out when those people played for that team.

Geologists use other tiny fossils in the same way. Conodonts are the teeth of small eel-like animals that swam in ancient oceans, and are very common in rocks from the ocean floor. They can also be collected very easily by dissolving the rocks in acid, which does not harm the conodonts. Like other microfossils, conodonts changed with time, so scientists can use them to date rocks.

Dates from conodonts and other microfossils are important because they count time in smaller chunks than the radioactive dating we mentioned in the last chapter. Counting radioactive atoms can give dates within 1 percent of the right time—but 1 percent of 100 million years is a million years. Microfossil dates can tell time in thousands of years, so they can tell much more about how fast the dinosaurs died. You can think of the fossil clock as a stopwatch with a minute hand that does not read hours, while radioactive dating is a separate clock with only an hour hand.

The geological clock has nothing quite like a second hand, but in a few rocks we can see things happening fairly fast—on a geological time scale. As the seasons cycle from summer to winter and back again, distinct layers form at the bottom of some lakes. Sometimes the clock can run even faster, when a flood or tsunami drops thick layers of material in days or hours. However, such layers are rare, and geologists can't count on finding many of them.

Fragmentary Evidence

Looking at fossils is somewhat like looking at the evidence of a crime, but there are some very important differences. In the United States it takes conclusive evidence to convict a person of a crime. A bloody fingerprint on the murder weapon would do the job. A footprint the same size as the suspect's in a yard three doors away would not. Scientists do not demand such conclusive evidence because they know they can't get it. The evidence does have to be consistent, but it need not be complete. Science works like a game in which the winner is the person who shouts the right answer first, and can make a good case why the answer is right.

Nor do scientists insist on having all the pieces of a fossil before they start talking about an animal. (If they did, they would have described very few fossils.) Instead, they fill in the missing pieces from their knowledge of other animals. This can cause mistakes. For many years, the brontosaurus skeleton in the American Museum of Natural History in New York wore the wrong skull. Scientists had found the skull near the brontosaurus skeleton, and, since it looked about right, they assumed it went with that skeleton.

Scientists have learned to live with the limits of the fossil record. For example, they can recognize fossil mammals by their teeth, which look different (at least to a specialist) for each type of mammal. In fact teeth are the only fossils we have of many early mammals, because teeth are much more durable than bones. The discovery of a single tooth in Australia produced headlines because it came from a type of mammal that scientists had thought never reached that part of the world.

Because there are so few fossil clues, scientists often point to the wrong suspects. They may get a bit red in the face when they discover their mistake, but that's part of the game of science. They know that as they find more evidence we will learn more about the causes of mass extinctions and of how they fit into the pattern of evolution.

4

Evolution: The Changing Face of Life

Fossil plants and animals differ from those that live today. That difference is strong evidence that life evolves from old forms into new ones. The evolution of living things is the framework for solving the puzzle of mass extinctions, like the life of a murder victim is a framework for solving a crime. The path of evolution also is changed by mass extinctions which may open the world to new creatures, like the death of the dinosaurs gave mammals a chance to evolve 65 million years ago.

The basic idea of evolution, as stated by Charles Darwin in 1859, is "natural selection," or "survival of the fittest." Animals may have many young, but only the best of them survive. The fittest rabbits would be those that could best escape from foxes, and the fittest foxes would be those that could catch the most rabbits. The change normally is very slow, over many generations.

The first horses, which lived 50 million years ago, were three-toed leaf-eating mammals about the size of a fox, called eohippus or hyracotherium. Over millions of years their descendants grew larger, and their feet evolved into one-toed hooves. As grasslands spread, they began eating grass and evolved teeth able to chew tough grasses. By adapting to a changing world, modern horses evolved the speed and long legs they needed for life on the plains.

We know many other examples of evolution. About the same time that eohippus roamed the land 50 million years ago, some larger mammals moved from the land into the sea. Gradually, their bodies grew larger and more streamlined, while their legs shrank. Their descendants are modern whales and dolphins, mammals that have adapted to life in the sea.

A few plants and animals have not changed much for a long time. Go back 300 million years, and you could find cockroaches, dragonflies, and horseshoe crabs that look much like modern ones. You would also find strange-looking reptiles with short, awkward legs, which have been extinct for over 200 million years. Descendants of those long-dead reptiles evolved into dinosaurs, modern lizards, snakes, birds, elephants, dinosaurs, and people. Animals that stay the same are exceptions, sometimes called "living fossils." Evolution is the rule.

Early Evolution

The first living cells were small and very simple things that lived 3.5 billion years ago. They apparently formed from large molecules in the oceans of the ancient earth. Later, some cells evolved into the first algae, which made their own food by capturing energy from the sun in what we call photosynthesis. Algae also produced oxygen as a waste product. Some oxygen combined with rocks or with salts in the ocean, but some stayed in the air, where it slowly changed the world.

Oxygen became common about two billion years ago. It was a deadly poison to many living things that had evolved earlier. Survival of the fittest meant survival of the cells that could tolerate oxygen. Those that could not live with oxygen died because of it. That may have been the first mass extinction, but we have no evidence of it.

Oxygen also opened doors for new evolution, because it let cells extract extra energy from their food so they could grow larger and more complex. Some single cells can live without oxygen, but most living things—from single-celled protozoa and tiny fungi to human beings—need oxygen to survive.

The next big evolutionary step was the emergence of animals with bodies containing many specialized cells. The oldest fossils of these animals are about 650 million years old. They were soft, bag-like creatures about half an inch (a centimeter) across, fixed to the ocean floor that probably ate algae that drifted into their hollow bodies. More complex animals evolved within tens of millions of years; like all soft-bodied animals they left very few fossils. Undersea mud slides 600 to 550 million years ago preserved impressions of jellyfish, segmented worms, and animals that look like old-fashioned quill pens. A few of these soft-bodied animals probably were ancestors of later animals, but others vanished. They may have been victims of a mass extinction, but the evidence is missing.

Hard Shells and Solid Evidence

Animals first evolved shells, which can be easily fossilized, about 540 million years ago, when life was confined to the oceans. Shells mark the start of the Cambrian period, a time when evolution shifted from slow motion into fast forward. Shells also give scientists the many fossils they need to trace the pattern of evolution.

The first shells were only a few millimeters (a small fraction of an inch) across. No one noticed these small fossil shells for many years, until Russian scientists looked very closely at rocks near the Siberian town of Tommot, which were just under the oldest rocks with obvious fossils. Soon other scientists around the world found similar fossils of the same age.

The tiny shells began a very busy 35 million years of evolution, like the start of spring after a long, cold winter. Many new animals appeared for the first time in the fossil record. Some vanished, but others evolved into modern animals. The most common Cambrian fossils were the shells of clam-like animals called brachiopods, and of segmented, many-legged animals called trilobites.

A fossil trilobite and a living fossil, the horseshoe crab. The 6.5-inch (16.5-centimeter) trilobite died 425 million years ago and was preserved in rock. (Courtesy of James Montanus / University of Rochester) *The horseshoe crab crawled out of this old shell, about the same size, which is turned upside down to show the crab's legs. The two are distant relatives of each other, and of spiders, scorpions, insects, crabs, and lobsters.*

Trilobites were related to insects and spiders, and their fossils look like wide, flat insects. They evolved rapidly into many different types that had the same basic structure, like all cars have four wheels, at least two seats, and an engine. And as carmakers introduce new models every year, evolution introduced new trilobite species frequently. A specialist in trilobites can tell the different species apart just as a car buff can spot different models and years. The common fossils of trilobites give good examples of evolution at work.

Many more shelly animals evolved after the trilobites, which faded away slowly and finally vanished about 245 million years ago. The fossil shells of these animals tell how evolution continued in the oceans. Fossil shells are so common that they are the best record of mass extinctions. Life on land is younger, and harder to study because it left fewer fossils.

The Move to Land

Plants reached the land first, over 420 million years ago. They had to change to survive on land. They had to evolve ways to control the flow of water within their stems, to avoid drying out, and to collect sunlight, minerals, and nutrients. The oldest fossil land plants were little more than twigs, but by about 360 million years ago, small trees had evolved.

Animals followed, and it was not easy for them, either. They had to keep water in their bodies to survive in the air. They couldn't swim on land, so they had to evolve new ways to move. They needed skeletons or shells sturdy enough to support their own weight. They also had to evolve eyes that could see in air and ears that could sense sound out of the water. Land and water are different worlds, and many animals live in only one. Crabs and their relatives rarely venture out of water or wetlands, and octopuses and their relatives all live in the sea. Insects have done very well on land, and a few live in fresh water, but none have returned to life in the sea. Later we will see that some mass extinctions had different effects on land and in the seas.

Animals which looked like spiders were the first animals to leave fossils on land; millipedes, scorpions and wingless insects were close behind.

By 350 million years ago, insects had evolved wings. Spiders, insects, and scorpions all are arthropods, with jointed legs and bodies covered by a thin, tough shell called an exoskeleton that supports their weight and keeps them from drying out. However, that design does not work well for larger animals.

Fish made their first big advance in the water about 400 million years ago, when they evolved jaws to catch other animals and fins to swim better. Some fish evolved strong, bony fins that could move them across the mud between drying ponds, and lungs that could gasp the air. Other fins worked better in water, but those fins evolved into legs that could walk on land. Fish evolved into amphibians, which grow from eggs laid in water and later live on land. They were the ancestors of all land animals with backbones, including reptiles, dinosaurs, pterosaurs, birds, and mammals.

Amphibians have internal bones, so they can grow much larger than insects; some reached alligator size. Reptiles evolved from amphibians. They do not dry out as easily, can lay their eggs on land, and walk better on land. Reptiles, in turn, evolved into several groups. Some became the reptiles we know today: turtles, crocodiles, snakes, and lizards. Others evolved into dinosaurs, mammals, pterosaurs, and extinct marine

Ichthyostega, one of the first amphibians, walks awkwardly on land with its newly evolved legs. (Courtesy of Doubleday, from C. L. Fenton, M. A. Fenton, P. V. Rich, and T. H. Rich, *The Fossil Book*)

reptiles that lived in the days of the dinosaurs. Dinosaurs, in turn, gave rise to the birds.

Mass extinctions helped shape evolution on land as well as in the oceans. Many amphibians and early reptiles died out 245 million years ago, at the end of the Permian period. Another extinction 202 million years ago, at the end of the Triassic, wiped out many reptiles, but left the land open for new generations of dinosaurs. Rodent-sized mammals had evolved by then, but they lived in the shadow of the dinosaurs. Dinosaurs ruled the land, marine reptiles ruled the seas, and pterosaurs ruled the air for 150 million years until they were wiped out by another mass extinction 65 million years ago at the end of the Cretaceous.

The death of the dinosaurs left the land to the survivors, the mammals and birds. They evolved rapidly in an empty world. All major groups of modern mammals evolved within 10 million years after the extinction.

Evolution and "Progress"

Evolution does not simply mean "progress." New animals are not any "better" than old ones, nor are mammals any "better" than reptiles or fish. Remember that the world is still full of simple single cells like those that evolved over a billion years ago and that many more fish than mammals live in the ocean.

Evolution really tries to match living things to their environment. Polar bears are white because that color hides them against Arctic snow and ice so that they can sneak up on their prey. Grizzly bears and black bears are dark to blend into the land where they live. Polar bears might not do well in the forest, and grizzly bears might not live long on the ice, but that does not mean that one is "better" than the other. It means that they evolved in different places.

The environment is not constant, forcing life to continue evolving. The world changes continually, although we do not always notice the changes. For the past two million years, the earth has had a series of cold ice ages, separated by warm spells called interglacials. We live in an interglacial period; 18,000 years ago, the sites of modern Boston,

Copenhagen, New York, Chicago, Minneapolis, and Moscow were covered by glaciers thousands of feet (over a kilometer) thick. Sea level has risen about 330 feet (100 meters) since then, drowning land that the first Native Americans crossed from Asia to Alaska. A vast inland sea that once covered central Utah has almost dried up, leaving only the shallow Great Salt Lake.

These continuing changes give evolution a moving target when it tries to adapt life to match the environment. If global warming melts the Arctic ice, polar bears must evolve to live in a warmer world, or face extinction. If the ice moves south, grizzlies will have to move or change.

The Balance of Life

The changing environment includes living things that themselves change. Some animals may evolve to take advantage of common plants. For example, some birds have beaks adapted to crack certain types of seeds—but they would be in trouble if the plants that produce the seeds were to disappear. Likewise, some plants come to depend on animals to spread their seeds. One tree on the Indian Ocean island of Mauritius evolved seeds with coats that could survive digestion by a dodo, but could not sprout otherwise, so that tree almost followed the dodo into extinction. Plants and insects also depend on each other in complex ways. Many plants need certain insects to pollinate their flowers; neither could survive without the other.

There are many other complex links among living things. Grass eaters like cattle and bison need grasslands to survive, and in return the animals help the grasslands. Grass leaves keep growing if you cut off their tops, but the leaves of other plants don't—which is why grass keeps growing after you mow it. Grazing animals eat other plants as well as the grass, but only the grass grows back. Take away the grazers, and in many places trees and bushes will cover the grassland after several years—just as they cover an abandoned pasture.

We can find many other ways in which living things shape their own environment. Animals use oxygen and produce carbon dioxide; plants use carbon dioxide and produce oxygen. The air must have both. Plants need carbon dioxide to grow; animals need oxygen to breathe. Nature has to balance both gases. If there is too much oxygen, the forests catch fire too easily; if there is too little, animals cannot survive. Carbon dioxide is a temperature control that keeps heat from escaping into outer space. Too much carbon dioxide makes the earth too hot, but too little might plunge the earth into another ice age.

Rocks absorb some oxygen and carbon dioxide from the air. Plants also take carbon dioxide from the air, and use the carbon it contains to grow leaves, stems, and roots. Eventually most plant matter is eaten or decays, but a little is buried underground, where it becomes coal, oil, or natural gas. When we burn those fossil fuels, we add carbon dioxide back to the atmosphere.

Somehow it has all stayed in balance for hundreds of millions of years. British scientist James Lovelock thinks this may not be an accident. He sees the entire planet as a living whole, which he calls Gaia (from the Greek word for Earth). He says that Gaia balances the levels of different gases, such as oxygen and carbon dioxide, in the atmosphere in order to keep the planet healthy. In other words, life itself keeps the earth the way it needs the planet.

The Gaia theory could explain some things that have puzzled scientists. The sun was dimmer in the past, but the oceans never froze solid. Perhaps life balanced the change in sunlight by changing carbon dioxide levels. The atmosphere does not seem to have changed too much since oxygen became abundant, although carbon dioxide levels probably have varied.

Living things may well have helped keep that balance—but scientists are not *certain*. Nor can we be sure that if there is a natural system, human actions will not throw it out of balance, causing serious problems.

How Does Evolution Work?

Evolution takes too long to see in a human lifetime. Evidence for evolution comes from fossils, which show that different plants and animals

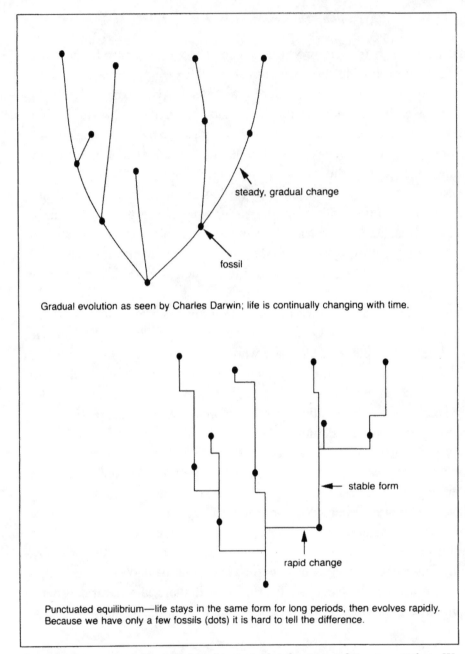

steady, gradual change

fossil

Gradual evolution as seen by Charles Darwin; life is continually changing with time.

stable form

rapid change

Punctuated equilibrium—life stays in the same form for long periods, then evolves rapidly. Because we have only a few fossils (dots) it is hard to tell the difference.

Scientists are not sure how living things evolve from one form to another. We can connect the dots (which represent fossils) by smooth lines, showing gradual evolution, or by zigzag lines, showing rapid change between long periods of stability, called punctuated equilibrium.

lived in the past, and from the plants and animals alive today. That evidence is good enough to convince almost all geologists and biologists that life evolves, but they do not agree as to how.

You can think of the fossil record as a connect-the-dots drawing. Each fossil is a dot, but there aren't many dots. The problem is to figure out how evolution connected the dots. Charles Darwin thought that plants and animals were always evolving slowly; he would have drawn smooth lines. He thought that missing links—animals that had evolved partway from one form to another—lay between the dots.

People looked hard for missing links, but most of them are still missing. That made other scientists wonder if the missing links really existed. Perhaps plants and animals evolve very fast for brief periods, but don't change at all the rest of the time, said Niles Eldridge and Stephen Jay Gould, who called their theory "punctuated equilibrium." For example, an animal might not change for a million years if the weather was warm, then evolve a thick fur coat in 10,000 years if the climate got much colder. So Eldridge and Gould would connect the dots with zigzag lines.

It is hard to prove which theory is right—if either one is. Life seems to evolve faster at some times than at others, but evolution may not stop between times. Perhaps each theory is true sometimes, or perhaps the truth really lies somewhere in between.

Mass extinctions fit better with the theory of rapid change. A dramatic change in the environment forces life to evolve rapidly to survive. If temperatures dropped suddenly, animals with the thickest fur would survive best, so their offspring would evolve thicker fur. Life could also evolve rapidly after a mass extinction, but for a different reason. Plants and animals could occupy new places in the environment, places formerly occupied by living things that had died out. That happened after the dinosaurs died, when mammals and birds evolved quickly into many different forms.

5

Assembling the Evidence

We can think of rocks and fossils as pieces of the mass extinction puzzle dumped onto a table. The challenge is to put it together. Knowing about evolution can help organize the evidence, like finding the edge pieces of a jigsaw puzzle. However, like detectives trying to solve a crime, scientists studying mass extinctions may not have all the evidence. We can't be sure that all the pieces we need are on the table, or that all the pieces on the table come from the same puzzle.

Scientists and detectives collect evidence and decide what it means. Detectives may interview people who were near the scene of the crime. They may read written records, such as bankbooks, diaries, telephone bills, or calendars. They look for physical evidence, like fingerprints or blood stains. They have to decide what is important and what isn't. Did the woman seen leaving the building at 6:00 commit the murder at 5:45, or did she just work in the office downstairs?

Mass extinctions are hard mysteries to solve. The evidence comes from the distant past, and the clues are not as easy to spot as bloody fingerprints on a murder weapon. In fact scientists first have to look for evidence that many animals or plants vanished suddenly, then look for more evidence to see what happened. *Was* there a mass extinction, and—if there was—what caused it?

44

The Fossils—Identifying the Victims

Fossils are the main evidence for mass extinctions. A big change in the fossils between two layers of rock means that a mass extinction may have happened. If nineteen out of twenty trilobite species vanish between two layers, the missing nineteen may have been victims of a mass extinction.

A big problem is that other events can leave the same evidence in the rocks. The old trilobites may have left the area because the environment changed, but they may have survived elsewhere. The younger rock may not have preserved fossils. A very common problem is a hiatus—the passage of a long time between formation of the two layers. Rocks may have stopped forming, or layers in between may have been eroded away before the upper rock formed. The two layers might be separated by millions of years, during which the trilobites could have died out slowly, without a mass extinction.

Scientists study mass extinctions by looking for fossils that are common, easy to find, and easy to recognize. They pick things like dinosaur teeth or the shells of ocean animals, not rare fossils like complete dinosaur skeletons. It's like counting cars on a highway; you do better if you look for Chevrolets than if you watch for Rolls Royces.

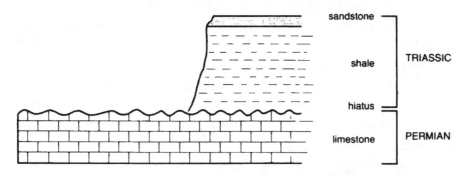

If rocks stop forming for a while, they leave a hiatus in the geologic record, shown here as a wavy line. Sea level dropped at the end of the Permian, exposing shallow seafloors. Some rocks washed away before the sea covered the area again and more rocks formed, leaving a hiatus between the Permian and the Triassic.

Most studies of mass extinctions have focused on shells from the bottoms of shallow seas. Scientists plot the layers where they find each species, looking for the last layer where each one appears. They use this data to count how many animals vanish in each interval of time. They may look at species, at genuses (groups of species) or families (in biology, groups of genuses).

The last fossil is not likely to be the last member of the species in the area, so it gives only a rough idea when the species really vanished. In fact the species may not have gone extinct; it may just have moved to another place, where it didn't leave fossils, like the coelacanth, a type of fish thought to be extinct for 80 million years until a living one was found deep in the Indian Ocean in 1938. However, if a species vanishes from the fossil record, scientists assume it went extinct.

Scientists organize fossil data to count how many species went extinct at different times. They plot a graph which shows how long different species lived. They find that many extinctions happen at certain times, while others are scattered. The times when many species seem to vanish are places to look for evidence of mass extinctions.

Survivors, Victims, and Newcomers

You can divide the fossils in two layers of rock into three groups. Some are survivors, present in both layers. Others are in the older layer but not in the younger, indicating the species had vanished, although not always forever. Still others are newcomers, in the younger rocks but not the older layer. Nature always has some coming and going, because change is part of evolution. Old species go extinct, new ones evolve, and a few return after seeming to vanish for a while. Mass extinctions are big changes; there are few survivors and many victims.

One way to approach the mass extinction mystery is to look for patterns in what survived and what didn't. Suppose you were looking at fossil fish from a small area. If all the victims were freshwater fish, and all the newcomers were ocean fish, you might suspect that salt water entered a freshwater lake or marsh.

Other patterns carry other messages. Many trilobites vanished from the warm shallow sea covering most of North America more than 500 million years ago. The new trilobites that replaced them had earlier lived in deeper, cooler water—a sign that the ocean may have cooled too much for the warm-water trilobites.

Other patterns appear in food chains. If plants disappear, the animals that eat them will vanish unless they find something else to eat. If plant-eating animals disappear, the meat eaters that prey upon them will also vanish, or will have to adapt to other food.

The number of fossils also conveys a message. If one group of trilobites simply replaced another, we would still see plenty of fossils. But if something killed all the old trilobites, others would take time to move into the empty regions, making fossils scarce for a while just after the extinction. If something killed the algae that supported the whole ocean food chain, animals like trilobites could not reappear until the algae returned. A long period of few fossils might indicate that life took a long time to recover from a big catastrophe—but it also might say that conditions changed, so fewer fossils were preserved.

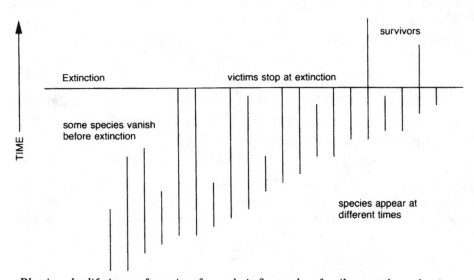

Plotting the lifetimes of species, from their first to last fossils, can show the time of a mass extinction.

Geography and Extinctions

Fossils tell us only what lived in the place where we find them. A species that vanishes from the fossil record may have moved because climate changed, or it may have been wiped out by a local disaster, like a flood or a volcanic eruption. It may have disappeared from a region because the sea grew too deep or too shallow for it. Sometimes animals vanish from whole continents but survive elsewhere. For example, horses died out in North America about 10,000 years ago, but survived in Europe and Asia. (Modern horses were brought to the Americas by Europeans.)

Scientists must check carefully to see that they do not mistake local events for mass extinctions. They look for rocks that formed about the same time in many different places. Similar patterns are evidence of mass extinctions. If a few places show extinctions, while others show nothing, the rocks probably record only local events.

It is not easy to find rocks the same age from many places. Rocks of certain ages are rare in some areas. In general, it gets harder to find rock the further back you go in time. Few rocks are known from certain times when sea level dropped, because that reduced the area where sediments could collect to form rocks.

Nor is it easy to be sure the rocks all formed at the same time. Rock layers are not the same everywhere. Geologists can date rocks that formed in the ocean by looking for common small fossils. However, it is hard to match rocks that formed on land and sea, because different plants and animals lived in each place. That makes it very hard to match the timings of extinctions on land and in the sea.

Geography also can affect extinctions. Species on a small island are more likely to die out than those on a large continent because there are fewer individual animals on the island. Changes in climate may affect different areas differently. If the world grows colder, animals from cool areas can move toward the equator, but those that live in the tropics may have no place left to go—so they may die out.

Remember, too, that the world itself has changed. The continents have moved. Two hundred fifty million years ago, Africa, South America, Australia, Antarctica, and India formed a single huge southern continent, Gondwana. Five hundred million years ago, much of modern North America and Greenland were a single continent that lay on its side along the equator—but Florida was part of Gondwana and lay near the South Pole. The world also has been much warmer through much of its history; just three million years ago, forests were growing along the coast of Greenland.

Events and Time Scales

The speed of mass extinctions can be an important clue as to what caused them. Did an impact or other catastrophe trigger a chain of events that killed most of the world's plants and animals? Might a series of events have happened over many years or centuries? Did the climate change over thousands or even millions of years?

Those questions are hard to answer because the geological clock usually ticks very slowly. Look at most rocks, and it's hard to tell if a change took place overnight or over the course of a thousand years. Only rarely do rocks form faster. A flash flood may deposit thick layers of dirt and rocks at the base of a mountain or in a floodplain. Geologists have found a handful of bone beds, containing skeletons of herds of animals caught by floods as they tried to cross streams. A tsunami may toss a thick layer of debris near the ocean shore. A volcano may deposit thick layers of ash or lava in an afternoon, then be quiet for hundreds of years.

If a great catastrophe caused a mass extinction, it might leave many clues behind. Suppose, for example, a huge rock from space splashed into the ocean, forming giant tsunamis that tumbled together tree trunks and rocks from the shore along with dirt and sand and other debris from the sea. Geologists can recognize tsunami deposits by looking at their layers: The big rocks settle out first, then lighter rocks, with sand and dirt on top. If a very thick tsunami deposit was just above the last rocks containing fossils of animals that became extinct, and there was other evidence of a space-rock impact, it might mean that an impact caused the extinctions.

Impacts also leave other evidence. The more unusual the evidence, the better it is for geologists, just as the police consider the butt of an expensive Cuban cigar to be better evidence than the filter of a common cigarette. Geologists search for three types of impact evidence:

• Tiny droplets of molten glass are formed when large impacts splatter melted surface rocks into the air. The drops of melted rock quickly become solid, forming tiny spheres of unusual dark glass called tektites, which land on the ground or in the ocean.

• The impact energy also shatters tiny quartz grains and throws them high into the atmosphere. The intense energy forms tiny cracks, called shock patterns, inside the grains, which geologists can see with special instruments.

• Finally, rocks from space contain some elements that are very rare on the surface of the earth. If a big enough rock hits, it can scatter those rare elements all over the planet. The best known of these elements is iridium, a heavy metal similar to platinum.

When geologists find layers that contain tektites, shocked quartz, or extra iridium, they suspect that these layers mark an impact. They must look in many places to see how large the impact was. A small impact would scatter tektites over only a small area, while a big one might leave extra iridium all over the planet. (In fact extra iridium scattered all over the globe by a big impact is a useful marker of all rocks formed at that time.)

Hidden Evidence

Scientists have found other evidence hidden in the rocks. The atoms and molecules in rocks can include "fingerprints" of living things and the environment where the rock formed.

One hidden clue is the two types of carbon atoms, called isotopes, found in old rocks. Most atoms are the lighter carbon-12 isotope, but 1.108 percent of all carbon atoms in nature are the heavier carbon-13.

Living things collect carbon-12 more efficiently, so rocks made from them (like coal) have extra carbon-12. This leaves other rocks, made from non-living things, with excess carbon-13. This makes carbon isotopes a clue to how many things were alive at the time these rocks were formed—the more they differ from the natural levels, the more abundant life was.

Oxygen in certain rocks is another hidden clue. Oxygen has three stable isotopes, which, like those of carbon, have different weights. Water containing the three isotopes freezes and boils at slightly different temperatures. This means that the ratios of the isotopes in the oceans changes with the temperature and with the amount of ice frozen on the surface of the earth. Shells and rocks from the ocean have the same ratios of oxygen isotopes as ocean water, giving scientists a rough thermometer of past ocean temperatures.

Assessing Evidence

Like detectives, scientists must look at all the evidence. They want to find enough pieces of the puzzle to solve the mystery. They also need to make sure all the evidence agrees.

Scientists have to be careful because their evidence is not conclusive. They are still arguing over whether all the dinosaurs vanished quickly or faded away over millions of years. They have even bigger questions about other mass extinctions. To try to understand what happened, they must bring together all the evidence they can find and see how it fits together.

So far, they have made the most progress on the extinction that killed the dinosaurs 65 million years ago. In the next three chapters, we will look at that extinction, the evidence it left, and its possible causes. Then we will look at other extinctions, from long ago until the present.

6

The Death of the Dinosaurs

The evidence is not what you might expect from a great dying. No thick layers of bones mark the end of the age of dinosaurs 65 million years ago. The most common tombstone for the dinosaur age is a thin layer of dark, barren rock, formed in shallow seas. Geologists call it the *boundary clay*. Clay is the stuff that makes up the rock, dark and fine-grained. The boundary is between two great eras of geologic time—the Mesozoic era of "middle life" and the Cenozoic era of "modern life."

The boundary has other names as well, for geologists have many names for blocks of time. It marks the end of the Cretaceous period, the third and last period in the Mesozoic era. It is sometimes called the Cretaceous-Tertiary (or K-T) boundary, because the Tertiary is one name for the period after the Cretaceous. Below the boundary layer are fossils from the dinosaur age; above it lie the first fossils from the age of mammals. The absence of dinosaurs is not the only difference between the layers. Spiral-shelled ammonoids, relatives of the squid and octopus, vanished from the sea, along with marine reptiles and clams that built giant reefs in shallow water. Pterosaurs and birds with teeth vanished from the air.

What killed them? I have asked that question of many scientists, and

Animals above the dashed line survived the mass extinction 65 million years ago; those below—ammonoids, marine reptiles, pterosaurs, and dinosaurs—did not. (Adapted from *Extinctions* by Steven Stanley, © 1987 by Scientific American Books. Reprinted by Permission.)

have gotten quite different answers. To find the best answers, we should review the evidence that they cite.

Counting Dinosaurs

A critical question about any extinction is, How fast did the victims die out? We can try to answer that question by counting dinosaur fossils in layers right up to the end of the Cretaceous. If the numbers do not change until the boundary, the dinosaurs must have died quickly, the victims of a sudden disaster or rapid change. A slow decline toward the boundary means the dinosaurs faded away gradually, perhaps the victims of climate change or competition from other animals.

The question isn't easy to answer because dinosaur fossils are rare, and there are few good sites to find them at the end of the Cretaceous. Scientists have counted dinosaur fossils, but their results don't agree. Some counts in some places show that dinosaurs were common until the very end of the Cretaceous. Other counts show that the number of dinosaur species dropped slowly, until only a few were left at the boundary.

What's wrong? You might think that counting dinosaur bones or dinosaur teeth should give the same results. It doesn't always work that way, just as sometimes the winning team in a baseball game has fewer hits than the losers. Perhaps the number of dinosaurs did not change much, but the number of species declined. Perhaps dinosaurs moved out of one area but stayed in others.

A big complication is that the best dinosaur fossils come from central North America, where the environment was changing at the end of the Cretaceous. A broad, shallow sea that had reached from Texas to the Canadian Arctic was drying up. Wet lowlands where dinosaurs had lived were shrinking. Those changes may have pushed dinosaurs out of the area, while they survived in other places.

Good dinosaur fossils from other regions might tell more about the end of the Cretaceous. We don't have the right fossils yet, but new discoveries outside of western North America have already brought some surprises. One is that the dinosaurs of western North America—triceratops, tyrannosaurs and the hadrosaurs—may not have been typical of the whole world. Western North America was a small, isolated continent during much of the Cretaceous, and, like modern Australia, its animals may have differed from those on other continents, says Thomas Holtz of the U.S. Geological Survey. For example, the big sauropod dinosaurs like brontosaurus left no fossils in western North

America for much of the Cretaceous. However, they remained on other continents, and a few returned to North America shortly before the end of the Cretaceous, apparently from South America.

We know that some dinosaurs survived until the very end of the Cretaceous, but we don't know how many. Answering that question is vital to solving the mystery of what happened to the dinosaurs. It would take a big disaster to kill many dinosaurs spread all over the world, but a small disaster could kill the last members of a dying breed. The answer will have to wait for new discoveries.

Could a few dinosaurs have survived past the Cretaceous? Scientists do not believe that every dinosaur died instantly, but we have no solid evidence that any survived very long after the Cretaceous. Some dinosaur teeth have been found in younger rocks, but they had been eroded from older rocks. Other claims of younger dinosaur fossils come from mistaken dating or identification. Almost no scientists believe claims that large dinosaur-like creatures still live in Loch Ness in Scotland or in a tropical African river.

Many other animals survived. Paleontologists David Archibald and Laurie Bryant cataloged thousands of fossils from animals in the Hell Creek formation in Montana. They counted 111 species of animals with backbones—more than half of which survived the end of the Cretaceous. Dinosaurs did not, but crocodiles did, making them the last of the *archosaurs,* or ruling reptiles, the group that includes the dinosaurs. Turtles also survived, as did smaller reptiles, amphibians, fish, mammals, and birds. Yet other relatives of the dinosaurs died at the same time. Pterosaurs vanished from the air and marine reptiles vanished from the sea. Freshwater animals seem to have done better than those that lived on land. We can learn something of what happened by comparing the victims with the survivors.

Pterosaurs and Birds

Pterosaurs were flying reptiles, their wings formed by thin membranes stretched between long finger bones. They must have evolved from ancient reptiles, but we do not know how. The first pterosaur fossils are about 220 million years old. Although the first pterosaurs look a bit awkward, they clearly could fly. Some were as small as songbirds, but as time passed they grew larger. They left fossils in rocks formed on land and sea throughout the dinosaur age. By the end of the Cretaceous, one giant pterosaur had wings that spanned 39 feet (12 meters), larger than some airplanes, making it the largest creature that ever flew.

Birds came later, evolving from small dinosaurs about 150 million years ago. Cretaceous birds included small tree-perching animals like modern songbirds, flying birds that looked somewhat like sea gulls, and flightless swimming birds somewhat like penguins. Many early birds had teeth.

Birds and pterosaurs shared Cretaceous skies. Some birds survived the great extinction, but no pterosaurs did. The fossil record tells us little about birds and pterosaurs in the late Cretaceous. The thin hollow bones that flying animals evolved to help them get off the ground are too fragile to leave many fossils.

We do know that fossil pterosaurs grew both rarer and larger during the Cretaceous. Only three of the nearly ninety known species of pterosaurs come from the late Cretaceous. One was the largest pterosaur ever, the 140-pound (65-kilogram) Quetzalcoatlus, which lived near the end of the Cretaceous and probably died with the dinosaurs. More common was the 37-pound (17-kilogram) pteranodon, with a wingspan of 23 feet (7 meters). The third species was smaller, but still larger than the small pterosaurs that lived earlier. Some specialists think birds had replaced small pterosaurs, and the giants were the last of a dying breed. Yet it's also possible that the small ones survived, but left no fossils that have yet been found.

Meanwhile, birds became more common in the late Cretaceous, although small bird fossils are very rare. The most common fossils are larger birds with teeth that lived in or near the sea, where their bones could fall to the bottom and become fossilized. Large toothed birds died out by the end of the Cretaceous, and may have been victims of the mass extinction. Smaller toothless birds survived the extinction; the oldest fossils of gulls, for example, come from the late Cretaceous.

Reptiles of the Sea

The mass extinction also wiped out the giant marine reptiles of the dinosaur era. Although some looked like dinosaurs, these animals evolved from different reptile families and were not true dinosaurs. They left many fossils, some beautifully preserved in soft silt at the bottom of quiet seas.

The fossils show some changes long before the end of the Cretaceous. Ichthyosaurs, which looked very much like dolphins, vanished about 80 million years ago, in the middle Cretaceous. Lizards moved into shallow seas about the same time and evolved into mosasaurs, streamlined giants up to 50 feet (15 meters) long. Mosasaurs stayed in shallow water and probably laid their eggs on land.

Other marine reptiles changed little from earlier times. Plesiosaurs had flippers like seals and may have crawled onto the shore like modern seals or sea lions. However, they were larger and looked more like dinosaurs with flippers than like whales or seals. One family, the Elasmosaurs, had long, snakelike necks and small heads that made them look like a seagoing version of brontosaurus—although they ate fish and other animals rather than plants. Another family, the Pliosaurs, had longer heads and shorter necks.

Both Plesiosaurs and Mosasaurs vanished at the end of the Cretaceous. They were probably victims of the mass extinction, but no fossils show that the big ocean reptiles survived until the very end of the Cretaceous.

Other Victims

The best evidence of sudden death at the end of the Cretaceous comes from the less-known victims. Microscopic fossil shells tell the clearest story. Some are thick in the rocks right up to the bottom of the boundary layer. There they stop. The animals had vanished.

The most common fossils are the hard shells of tiny single-celled plants and animals that floated in the ocean. As we saw in chapter 3, each has a unique shape, which experts can recognize. Normally these tiny fossils changed slowly, with each species living about a million years. Something different happened at the end of the Cretaceous. Almost all tiny shells that are common just below the boundary layer are missing from the rocks just above it. Only a handful of these species survived. New types start appearing later. It looks as if something wiped out most of the tiny plants and animals at the end of the Cretaceous.

Many larger ocean animals also stopped leaving fossil shells at the end of the Cretaceous. Small clams that grew in large groups, and had built great reefs during the Cretaceous, vanished totally. Many snails also vanished. So did many corals, which built reefs in shallow water.

One striking loss was the ammonoids. Relatives of the octopus and squid, they lived in elaborate spiral shells, which make beautiful fossils. Like the octopus and squid, they squirted jets of water to push themselves through the sea. They had evolved over 300 million years earlier and had recovered from other mass extinctions. They did not survive whatever happened at the end of the Cretaceous.

Many scientists long thought the ammonoids had faded away before the end of the Cretaceous. In most places, their fossils are missing from rocks just below the boundary layer. However, after years of searching, Peter Ward of the University of Washington found rocks along the Bay of Biscay that told a different story. Many ammonoids were less than a yard (a meter) below the boundary layer, clear evidence that some ammonoids had survived until the very end of the Cretaceous.

Why were ammonoid fossils missing from other rocks? Ward thinks that ammonoids had left shallow water to escape predators that could crush their shells. The rocks he found had formed in water too deep for the predators. It was a refuge for the ammonoids, but it could not save them from extinction.

Survivors

Comparing survivors and victims also gives us evidence about the extinction. At Hell Creek the dinosaurs were wiped out, and many lizards and sharks vanished (perhaps because the area became dryer). Most mammals, turtles, and amphibians in that area survived, however. Paleontologist Peter Sheehan, who took his own look at the Hell Creek fossils, found that land animals were hit hard, but animals that lived in fresh water survived best. He thinks the water animals may have survived because they have different diets. While land animals eat fresh plant and animal food, water animals eat debris they find floating in the water.

Around the world, the most obvious trend was that small animals survived but big ones did not. Nothing that weighed more than about 50 pounds (25 kilograms) is known to have lived through the extinction. Some scientists estimate the limit as low as 10 pounds (5 kilograms). The big animals, the giant reptiles of land and sea that left many fossils behind, all died. But many smaller animals lived.

Crocodiles, turtles, lizards, and snakes all outlived the dinosaurs. Mammals, tiny creatures that had hidden from the thundering steps of the great dinosaurs, also survived. So did birds, but probably not the largest ones, which left the most fossils in the Cretaceous. Few land plants went extinct.

The survivors inherited a world without giants. They quickly spread all over the planet, and evolved to fill the places left open by the death of the dinosaurs. The major modern groups of birds and mammals evolved in the first 10 million years after the end of the Cretaceous. Some birds grew taller than a person and some mammals grew even larger, but on land they never reached the bulk of the dinosaurs. Only at sea did mammals become true giants—the blue whale is the largest living creature known.

Other Evidence

Dead bodies are not the only evidence of murders. The killers may leave other clues. Both detectives and geologists look for things out of the ordinary, hoping they might tell something about what happened. Geologists have found some unusual things in rocks formed at the end of the Cretaceous.

Thick layers that look as if they were formed by a giant tsunami mark the end of the Cretaceous in a few places around the Caribbean and the Gulf of Mexico. The deposits formed near ancient coasts—some in shallow water, some deeper in the sea. They contain an odd mixture of things, from fossilized logs and branches to rocks that formed offshore. They include large chunks of rock that would have taken tremendous energy to move. They indicate that something big happened in the ocean, but they don't prove anything by themselves.

All around the world, rocks formed at the end of the Cretaceous contain more than the usual amount of iridium. Iridium is very rare on the surface of the earth; less than one in every ten billion atoms in normal rock is iridium. However, iridium is much more common in the boundary clay, which in some places contains up to a thousand times the normal level. Something must have sprinkled the earth with extra iridium at the end of the Cretaceous.

The boundary layer also contains small grains of quartz with unusual microscopic flaws inside them. Quartz is a very common rock; it supplies most of the sand on beaches. The flaws are what is strange. They are formed only when the quartz crystals are "shocked" by something hitting them very hard. A big volcanic explosion can produce some flaws, but the shocked quartz in the boundary clay was hit by something more powerful than a volcano.

In some places the boundary clay also contains tiny dark tektites. They formed when molten rock splashed into the air and cooled so quickly it became a glass.

Layers just above the boundary clay have other secrets hidden in them. Some are very rich in soot—as if vast forests had burned. Some contain

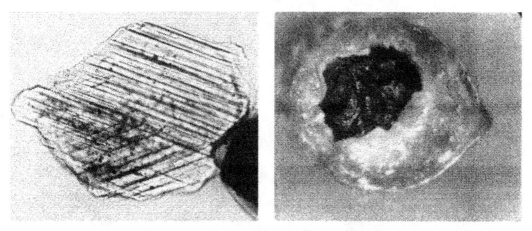

Shocked quartz (left) *and a tektite* (right) *from the end of the Cretaceous; the light outer layer of the tektite has turned to clay but the inside is dark glass.* (Courtesy of Glen Izett / U.S. Geological Survey)

much more pollen from ferns than from any other kind of plant. And for many years after the extinctions, many rocks seem to show that the oceans had much less life than during the late Cretaceous.

No one of these unusual bits of evidence proves what happened at the end of the Cretaceous. None are as convincing evidence as a bloody fingerprint on a murder weapon. But they are part of a pattern that points to a most likely cause, which we will talk about in the next two chapters.

7

Theories of Extinction

Now that we've listed the evidence, we can take a hard look at theories of what happened at the end of the Cretaceous. Like detectives trying to solve a murder, we must search for suspects and more evidence to prove our case. We should also keep our eyes open for suspects in other mass extinctions, described in later chapters.

The Cretaceous extinction mystery started as a simpler question: What happened to the dinosaurs? In the nineteenth century, some people thought the dinosaurs drowned in the biblical flood. Others thought they might survive in some remote corner of the world. Now we know that the whole world changed 65 million years ago. What really happened, and why? I have heard many different theories.

Slow or Fast Extinctions

We can sort ideas about mass extinctions into two broad groups. One group blames slow natural changes in the environment, such as global cooling, global warming, or the evolution of competing animals or predators. The other blames global disasters of various types.

For many years geologists assumed the dinosaurs died slowly. That was only natural because modern geology is based on the idea that the earth has always changed the same way it does today—very slowly. Scientists could not imagine a catastrophe that could devastate the entire world. All the disasters they knew—earthquakes, volcanoes, floods, and tsunamis—fell far short. An earthquake might shatter buildings in a whole city, but not around the world. A volcanic eruption might destroy an island, but not a continent.

Most geologists now think global disasters could have happened, but they do not agree on how many extinctions they caused. A few think global catastrophes caused most extinctions, while some think disasters only killed animals that were already in trouble. A few others doubt that disasters caused many extinctions at all. The one thing everyone agrees on is that the picture is complicated.

Gradual Extinctions

For many years, scientists thought dinosaurs were sluggish, stupid, and cold-blooded animals. Other reptiles are cold-blooded, so they run out of energy quickly and must warm in the sun on cool days. Dinosaurs had small brains for their sizes; stegosaurus is legendary for having a brain the size of a walnut. Mammals are smaller, but smarter, faster, and more "advanced," if you think of evolution as a type of progress— as many scientists did well into this century. It seemed only natural to think that the smart young mammals had driven the dumb old dinosaurs to extinction.

We now know it was not that simple. The first mammals evolved at almost the same time as the dinosaurs, about 230 million years ago. They lost their first chance to conquer the world. The dinosaurs evolved to be giants; the mammals stayed small, living in the shadows of the dinosaurs for over 150 million years. Many scientists now think the dinosaurs were fast-moving, warm-blooded creatures. If they didn't have much in the way of brains, they seemed to survive perfectly well without them, like the scarecrow in *The Wizard of Oz*. The mammals benefited from the death of the dinosaurs, but we can't blame them for it.

Some other ideas also did not work out. One was that dinosaurs could not digest the flowering plants that evolved during the Cretaceous—but flowering plants evolved long before the dinosaurs died. Another idea was that the dinosaurs ran out of genetic energy and faded away. However, no one can think why that should happen, and a few animals—like dragonflies and horseshoe crabs—have survived much longer than the dinosaurs.

Changing Environments

What else might have killed the dinosaurs slowly? Changes in the environment are the most likely possibility. The earth's climate changes slowly on a human scale, but it can change dramatically on a geological scale. Just 18,000 years ago, thick ice sheets covered the sites of modern New York, Boston, Detroit, and London, and a huge lake, hundreds of feet deep, filled the Great Salt Lake Basin in Utah. That ice will probably come back some day if people don't make the world too warm.

Many things can change climate. Small variations in the earth's orbit cause the ice to advance and retreat about every one hundred thousand years. Changes in ocean currents when the Isthmus of Panama rose above sea level three million years ago may have helped start the ice ages. Central North America dried out as mountains rose along the west coast; the great Himalayas shape the climate of Asia. Over tens of millions of years, the continents move from one climate zone to another. Australia dried out as it moved north into the same arid zone that dries the deserts of Namibia and Botswana in Africa.

The earth was very warm during the Cretaceous. Dinosaurs lived in Alaska, which was a little closer to the North Pole than it is today. Wyoming was tropical. Cooling near the end of the Cretaceous may have caused problems for plants and animals that had evolved in a warm climate.

Sea level also changed. It was very high in the Cretaceous, covering large areas on the continents. For millions of years a shallow sea divided North America into two parts, keeping the center of the continent warm

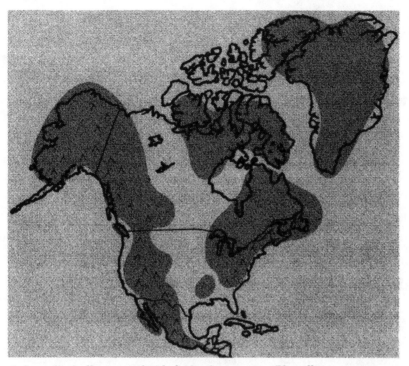

A broad, shallow sea divided North America 70 million years ago, leaving only the shaded areas above water. Did the drying up of this sea push dinosaurs toward extinction?

and humid. The sea began retreating in the late Cretaceous as sea level dropped and the middle of the continent began rising. This changed the whole midcontinental environment. Coastal wetlands and swamps dried, threatening plants and animals that had evolved along the shores. The drop in sea level left coastal lowlands dry around the world.

We will see in later chapters that the earth's climate has changed at the times of other mass extinctions. The changes at the end of the Cretaceous may have caused some extinctions. However, other events at the end of the Cretaceous do not fit neatly into the pattern of slow change.

When Worlds Collide

The face of the moon shows many craters, the scars of four billion years of comet and asteroid impacts. The moon is cold and geologically dead, so nothing wears away old craters. But asteroids and comets still wander the solar system, and a few cross the earth's orbit. Could they hit our planet?

The earth is a much larger target than the moon, and its much stronger gravity should pull more objects toward it. But its surface shows very few obvious craters. The reason is that the earth is an active planet. Water and wind wear away craters like they wear down mountains. Plate motion destroys old ocean crust and crumples continents together. Sediment buries some old craters. Impacts happen, but time obscures the craters.

The best example of a young crater is the Barringer Meteor Crater in the Arizona desert. If you know what you're looking for, you can sometimes see it from a plane flying over Flagstaff, Arizona. About 4,000 feet (1,200 meters) across, it was formed tens of thousands of years ago by the impact of a 300-foot (90-meter) nickel-iron meteor— roughly the size of one of the Egyptian pyramids. Geologists have found many other older and larger craters, but none are as obvious from the air. The south German town of Nördlingen lies in the best-preserved large crater, the 16-mile (26-kilometer) Ries Crater, formed 15 million years ago. A ring-shaped lake sits in the 40-mile (70-kilometer) Manicouagan Crater in Quebec, formed more than 200 million years ago.

Some objects explode in the atmosphere, leaving no crater, but the blast can do tremendous damage. On the morning of June 30, 1908, a 100-foot (30-meter) object exploded about six miles (ten kilometers) over the Tunguska River in Siberia. The blast flattened trees over an area of about 800 square miles (2,000 square kilometers) that fortunately was not inhabited. For many years scientists thought a comet caused the Tunguska explosion, but a new study indicates that it may have been a rocky meteor.

The larger the object, the more the damage. Scientists trying to un-

Barringer Meteor Crater, near Flagstaff, Arizona. (Courtesy of U.S. Geological Survey)

derstand the end of the Cretaceous have calculated effects of an impact by a 6-mile (10-kilometer) asteroid. Even before the object hit the ground, its energy would have split air molecules, converting nitrogen and oxygen into nitrogen oxides. That would have made acid rain as strong as the acid in an automobile battery near the impact. It would have burned the leaves off the trees and the skins off the animals hiding beneath them. It would have made the upper layer of the ocean strongly acidic, killing the plants and animals that lived there. The acid rain would have been weaker farther away from the impact, but still harmful.

A 6-mile (10-kilometer) object would have formed a crater about 100 miles (150–200 kilometers) across. It would have splattered molten rock droplets from the target area high into the air. Larger chunks of rock would have been strewn across wide areas near the impact site, like drops of water when a rock splashes into a pool. The blast would have been heard around the world and would have shaken the whole earth. If the object had hit an ocean, it would have raised a gigantic splash— a tsunami as high as the ocean was deep. That giant wave would have

COMETS AND ASTEROIDS

The earth's upper atmosphere is constantly bombarded by tiny grains of interplanetary dust and small pebbles, but they burn up in the air. Only larger objects—comets and asteroids—can cause devastating impacts.

Most comets stay beyond the orbit of Pluto, but a few come into the inner solar system. When they come close to the sun, the frozen gases they contain boil off the surface, forming bright white tails up to millions of miles long. However, most of the mass is in the nucleus, a ball of ice and rock a few miles (several kilometers) across. Very few comets are spectacular, and all are hard to see in cities and towns with bright lights. The earth has passed through comet tails without effect, and small chunks of cometary material probably would explode harmlessly high in the atmosphere. However, a big comet nucleus could hit the ground.

Asteroids contain more rock and metal than comets, and do not produce gas when they approach the sun. The largest, Ceres, is 600 miles (1,000 kilometers) across, but most are much smaller, about the size of a comet nucleus. Many asteroids may be burned-out comets, with some ice left in the cores, protected by layers of dirt and rock. Others may be mostly rock or metal. Most stay between Mars and Jupiter, but a few cross the orbit of Earth.

It is hard to tell if asteroids or comets formed particular impact craters. While small chunks of comets should explode high in the atmosphere, a comet nucleus a few miles across should hit the ground as hard as a rocky asteroid. The main difference seems to be that asteroids contain much more iridium than comets. That makes an asteroid a better suspect for the K-T impact.

devastated coasts and torn at things living near the ocean surface, throwing some into the air and pulling others deep underwater.

The impact would have thrown huge amounts of dust and tiny droplets high into the atmosphere, where they would have blocked sunlight and cooled the planet's surface for months or longer. It would have been the sudden start of an impact winter. Plants, cold and starved of sunlight, would have stopped growing and died. Animals that ate live plants would have starved or frozen in the cold. Scavengers would have feasted, briefly, until they had devoured all the dead plant-eaters. Then they, too, would have starved.

At sea the darkness would have killed the microscopic plants in the surface layer. Marine animals would have starved, because they depend on the tiny plants for food. Animals near the ocean bottom might have survived by feeding on the debris drifting down from the great dying.

Global biomass—the total amount of living things—would have dropped dramatically in months. As the air cleared, more light would have reached the surface, warming the ground. Seeds would have sprouted after a sleep of months or years. Ferns would have grown first, just as they do in the open spaces left by forest fires or volcanic eruptions. Weeds would have followed, and, in time, trees.

Some scientists are amazed that anything could have survived such an impact. The world would have taken many years to recover. Burn an ancient forest, and hundreds of years pass before the new forest looks like the old one. It might take even longer after a severe impact winter. Plants can recover because their seeds can survive through years of cold and darkness. Animals would have had a harder time because they have no dormant stages like seeds that could survive without food for months or years. The giants probably would have starved first in the devastated world, going extinct for lack of a refuge. Small animals and scavengers would have had a better chance to survive because they needed less food or could survive by eating debris from the great dying.

Small animals also would have a better chance because there were more of them. If only one mouse in 10,000 survived, the species would not go extinct, because there were untold millions of mice. The same odds would doom bigger and rare animals like the elephant and rhinoceros.

The oceans, too, would be slow to recover. Plants and algae could have survived if they had dormant stages, like the seeds of land plants or the spores of bacteria. Large animals would have died, while the small and the scavengers would have had the best chance of living. As the light returned, plants would have bloomed again on the surface, but it would have taken time for life to recover, especially if the surface waters stayed strongly acidic.

The impact theory matches much evidence from the end of the Cretaceous. Asteroids contain more iridium than the earth's surface, so an impact could have spread the excess iridium found in the boundary layer. Impacts can also form shocked quartz and tektites. The patterns of extinction also come close to what scientists find at the end of the Cretaceous. But there are other ideas.

Volcanoes

It doesn't take an impact to put dust high into the air and cool the earth. The 1991 explosive eruption of Mount Pinatubo in the Philippines blew millions of tons of dust and tiny droplets of sulfuric acid into the upper atmosphere. That debris scattered sunlight, giving us brilliant sunsets—and cooling the planet 1 to 2 degrees Fahrenheit (.5 to 1 degree Celsius) the following summer. The 1815 eruption of Tambora in Indonesia threw about ten times more dust and droplets into the upper atmosphere, and the next year was so cold that it was called "the year without a summer."

Much larger eruptions have happened in the past. A huge crater in Sumatra was formed 73,400 years ago by the eruption of 670 cubic miles (2,800 cubic kilometers) of molten rock and vapor—more than five hundred times larger than Pinatubo. That could have cooled the world 7 to 10 degrees Fahrenheit (4 to 5 degrees Celsius) for several years—devastating indeed.

The most gigantic lava flows in the geologic record come from different types of volcanoes, located over "hot spots" like the one that formed

Mount Pinatubo erupts in 1991. (Courtesy of David H. Harlow / U.S. Geological Survey)

the Hawaiian Islands. Instead of exploding, these volcanoes pour hot molten lava onto the land. They put less of their material into the air—but the eruptions are immense. The largest have ejected over 240,000 cubic miles (a million cubic kilometers) of lava in a series of eruptions spanning at least thousands of years. That's enough to cover the entire state of California with 1.5 miles (2.4 kilometers) of rock.

Such tremendous eruptions probably changed the climate. Their timing also looks very suspicious. Two of the largest eruptions happened close to severe mass extinctions. About 360,000 cubic miles (1.5 million cubic kilometers) of lava covered what is now southwestern India about 65 million years ago, at the end of the Cretaceous. And some 480,000 cubic miles (2 million cubic kilometers) of lava covered parts of Siberia about 245 million years ago, at the time of the extinctions described in chapter 9.

Two geologists from Dartmouth College, Charles Officer and Charles Drake, have argued for years that the Indian eruptions caused the extinctions at the end of the Cretaceous. The evidence does show signs of a catastrophe 65 million years ago, but it doesn't look as if it was the volcanoes that killed the dinosaurs. The fingerprints don't match. The Indian rocks contain very little iridium; asteroids contain plenty. Volcanoes cannot make the shocked quartz crystals found in rocks from the end of the Cretaceous. An impact best fits the evidence for that extinction, but that does not mean that volcanoes had nothing to do with any other extinctions.

Weighing Evidence

It is not easy to deduce the events of millions of years ago. Some evidence suggests that gradual change caused the extinctions at the end of the Cretaceous. Other evidence points to a catastrophe. Scientists have spent the last decade looking for the crucial "smoking gun"—an impact crater from the end of the Cretaceous.

We'll talk about the great crater hunt in the next chapter. It makes for a fascinating story, but just finding the crater does not solve the mass extinction mystery. The global environment had been changing before the Cretaceous ended. An impact might not have killed the dinosaurs by itself. Perhaps they were already fading away, and the impact just pushed them over the edge a bit early—like a man with a weak heart who suffers a fatal heart attack when someone points a gun at him.

8

The Great Cretaceous Crater Hunt

The great Cretaceous crater hunt began as a father-son project. The father was Luis Alvarez of the Lawrence Berkeley Laboratory in Berkeley, California, who won the 1968 Nobel Prize in physics for studying particles smaller than atoms. The son was Walter Alvarez, a young geology professor at the University of California at Berkeley. Wanting to find a problem they could work on together, the Alvarezes decided to measure how fast sediments had formed at the end of the Cretaceous.

It didn't seem like a big problem in the mid-1970s, but it was one in which their interests and skills overlapped. Walter Alvarez thought they could tell how fast sand and silt had settled to the ocean floor by looking in the rocks for elements like iridium, which are much more common in meteor dust than on the earth's surface. Luis Alvarez had instruments to make the measurements. The two found rocks of the right age near Gubbio, Italy, and sent them back to Berkeley.

They got a surprise. Walter Alvarez had thought that silt had collected slowly at the end of the Cretaceous. He had expected to find two to three times more iridium than normal, because the slow-forming rock had extra time to collect more iridium-rich meteor dust. The laboratory measured iridium levels *thirty* times normal.

Luis and Walter Alvarez at Gubbio; the light rock is the Cretaceous-Tertiary boundary layer. (Courtesy of the University of California at Berkeley)

Something strange had happened. Where had the extra iridium come from? They checked rocks formed in other places at that same time, and found they also contained too much iridium. Something had scattered the rare metal all over the earth. The Alvarezes decided that an asteroid may have hit the planet. Knowing how much iridium meteorites contained, they calculated that a 6-mile (10-kilometer) asteroid could have supplied the extra iridium.

That big an object would make a crater 90 to 120 miles (150 to 200 kilometers) across. It would have caused a global disaster, perhaps including the mass extinctions that ended the Cretaceous. The Alvarezes chased down the loose ends and wrote a paper for the journal *Science*. It caught my eye, and the attention of many scientists, and started the great crater hunt.

A Hole as Big as Connecticut

Many scientists were at first very skeptical. They had thought that the dinosaurs had died out slowly. Besides, the crucial "smoking gun" was missing—the crater. The Alvarezes expected to find a hole as big as Connecticut, and you would think that would be very hard to hide. Yet no crater of the right age and right size shows on the earth's surface. The circular ring of Lake Manicouagan in Quebec is only about 40 miles (70 kilometers) across, and it is far too old. The 60-mile (100-kilometer) Popigai Crater in the Siberian Arctic is too young. The Alvarezes said that the crater might be hidden under the ocean or might have been destroyed by plate motion in the last 65 million years. The skeptics didn't accept those ideas.

Other scientists, however, were finding evidence that something big had happened at the end of the Cretaceous. They found extra iridium all over the planet. In fact scientists now use excess iridium to identify the end of the Cretaceous. They also found shocked quartz and tektites in rocks formed at the same time in and near North America. Both are produced only by impacts.

Other evidence also pointed to a disaster, like a layer rich in soot found close to the iridium in many places. Edward Anders of the University of Chicago thought the soot came from vast forest fires. An impact could have ignited fires that destroyed the trees, or trees killed by the darkness after an impact could have burned later. Above the soot is a layer rich in fern spores, just what would grow in soil left after global forest fires.

It all looked as if an impact might have happened. But where was the crater?

The Manson Crater

Throughout the 1980s, geologists searched the earth for signs of craters, then tried to date them. They found some craters under soil and other rocks, but not until 1988 did they find anything that was about the right age. It lay in the prairie near Manson, Iowa, hidden by 100 feet (30 meters) of soil and rocks left by the last ice age.

The Manson Crater is invisible from the surface. It was found in the 1960s, when people drilling wells for water came up with some unusual shattered rocks. Geologists probed the area and found an oval pattern 25 by 18 miles (40 by 29 kilometers), which looked like a buried crater. In 1988 Mick Kunk of the U.S. Geological Survey dated rocks from the crater at 65 million years old, matching the end of the Cretaceous.

Some geologists quickly hailed the Manson Crater as the "smoking gun" proving an asteroid impact at the end of the Cretaceous. The crater was as big as a major city. It fit with other evidence that the impact was in or near North America. The problem was that Manson was much smaller than the Alvarezes had predicted—probably too small to cause global extinctions. Manson was a "smoking pistol," said Gene Shoemaker of the U.S. Geological Survey, but the "smoking cannon" was still missing.

A Caribbean Tsunami

The Manson Crater also did not match another key piece of evidence found at about the same time—a thick layer of rocks along the Brazos River in Texas formed at the end of the Cretaceous. At the bottom were large stones tumbled together, with smaller and smaller rocks above them, and finally a layer of sand and fine silt. Joanne Bourgeois of the University of Washington studied the rocks and said they were formed by a huge Caribbean tsunami when that part of Texas lay along the shore.

An ocean impact would have caused a tsunami. A shallow sea may have covered Manson at the time, but an impact there would not have made a tsunami big enough to reach Texas. Bourgeois's discovery pointed crater hunters toward the Caribbean. It was a vital clue that came at the right time.

In October 1988, some two hundred scientists met at the Snowbird ski resort in Utah to discuss global catastrophes and mass extinctions.

It was a time for them to share their findings and talk about their ideas. I covered the meeting for *New Scientist* magazine. Luis Alvarez had died a month earlier, but I heard Anders, Walter Alvarez, Bourgeois, Kunk, Shoemaker, and many others talk about their work. They puzzled over what the evidence might mean. They argued over how fast the extinctions had happened and whether to blame volcanoes, asteroids, or something else. Caught up in the excitement, I filled three notebooks and stayed up late talking with the scientists. It sounded as if they were getting closer to an answer.

Among the people who talked at Snowbird was Alan Hildebrand, then a graduate student at the University of Arizona. Finding the crater was his thesis project. Manson wouldn't do—he wanted the big one, Shoemaker's "smoking cannon." Hildebrand was already looking at the Caribbean, and he arrived at Snowbird with a couple of ideas as to where a crater might be hidden. They didn't convince many people.

The Caribbean Connection

Many scientists went home from Snowbird with ideas for new projects. Hildebrand went home to look for other evidence of a Caribbean impact. He searched through old research papers and contacted other scientists. He hit pay dirt when he spoke to Florentin Maurrasse, a native of Haiti and expert on Caribbean geology who is a professor at Florida International University in Miami. Maurrasse had earlier found thick layers of disturbed rocks in Haiti. At first he thought they were formed by volcanic eruptions at the end of the Cretaceous. Later he looked closer and found tektites and tiny crystals of shocked quartz— evidence of an impact. He also found that the rocks contained 1 to 3 feet (.3 to 1 meter) of shattered ocean crust, a sign that the impact had taken place nearby.

Maurrasse knew of thick layers of broken rock called brecchias in the Dominican Republic, Cuba, and Jamaica that were about the same age. They looked like debris from a nearby impact. His knowledge of the area helped put together more pieces of the puzzle. However, plate motion has scrambled the Caribbean in the past 65 million years, so rocks on the islands do not point directly to an impact site.

Ironically the crucial piece of the puzzle had been found years before, but was put aside because no one realized what it was. In 1978 geologist Glen T. Penfield surveyed the Yucatán coast for the Mexican national oil company, Pemex. He found signs of a peculiar ring about 110 miles (180 kilometers) across and .6 mile (1 kilometer) underground. Pemex geologists had noticed it earlier, but thought it was volcanic. Penfield thought it looked like a crater from the end of the Cretaceous, and told Carlos Byars, a writer who then worked for the same company. It took a long time for Penfield to persuade Pemex to let him talk about the crater, and then it was only to talk to a group of oil specialists who didn't really care. However, Byars had gone to work for the *Houston Chronicle,* and he wrote about the crater for the newspaper in 1981. Nobody paid much attention to that, either.

Byars asked other scientists about the Yucatán crater, but none were interested, until he met Hildebrand. Byars put Hildebrand in touch with Penfield, and the two compared notes. They chased down pieces of rock Pemex had drilled from the site in 1951. A fire had destroyed most of the rocks, but they found enough pieces to see that the structure was a crater of exactly the right age. Its center is close to the Mexican coastal town of Progreso. Penfield named the structure Chicxulub after a nearby village; the name means "the devil's tail" in the native Mayan language.

The rocks at Chicxulub record an impact in 600 to 1,000 feet (200 to 300 meters) of ocean water by a 6-mile (10-kilometer) asteroid. The impact energy vaporized ocean water and rock, digging a crater a couple of thousand feet (several hundred meters) deep in the ocean floor. The splash was a giant tsunami. Normally a tsunami can be only as tall as the water is deep, but the tremendous shock from the impact may have caused underwater landslides that produced other large tsunamis. The gigantic waves must have devastated Caribbean coasts; other tsunami deposits have been found in Mexico. The impact left a hole as big as Connecticut. If a freeway ran straight across it, the drive would take two hours, nonstop.

Chicxulub Crater lies along the Yucatán coast. Partly submerged today, the area was covered by shallow seas at the end of the Cretaceous.

The gigantic impact also threw dust and vaporized rock high into the atmosphere. Some dust and vapor came from the asteroid, but most came from the rocks it hit. Glen Izett of the U.S. Geological Survey says the target rocks may have made the disaster much worse. The asteroid hit a thick bed of limestone rich in a mineral called *anhydrite*, calcium sulfate. Vaporize calcium sulfate and water, and you produce tiny droplets of sulfuric acid. Some droplets would have added to the strong acid rain after the impact. Others would have been thrown high into the atmosphere.

Tiny droplets and dust grains scatter light. If they are high in the air, some light goes into space, cooling the earth. Dust drifts down in weeks or months. The tiny sulfuric acid droplets can stay in the upper atmosphere for a couple of years. The 1991 eruption of Mount Pinatubo cooled the earth roughly a degree. Chicxulub did much worse, throwing the world into a deep, dark impact winter.

Heat may have followed. The impact must have released carbon dioxide from the calcium carbonate in limestone. Carbon dioxide is what we call a greenhouse gas, because it lets sunlight reach the surface, but traps heat from the planet. The extra carbon dioxide from the impact could have made the earth too hot, killing some plants and animals that survived the darkness.

In time the world settled down. Calm tropical ocean once again covered the Yucatán, including the crater. Over millions of years, a slow rain of tiny shells buried the crater under up to 3,000 feet (1 kilometer) of limestone. Some of the region rose above sea level. Today, half the structure is still covered by shallow water along the Yucatán coast; the other half is on dry land. Satellite photos show a ring of ponds about 110 miles (180 kilometers) in diameter on the land side, where water has seeped through the shattered rock. That's what the Alvarezes predicted.

How Many Impacts?

If Chicxulub is the smoking cannon, what is Manson? The two craters are about the same age. Shoemaker and Izett think the two impacts came fairly close together, but certainly not on the same day. Izett says he has found two separate impact layers in many areas of western North America. He thinks Chicxulub formed the lower one and Manson the upper one. He doesn't know how much time passed between them, but in some places plant roots grew through the intermediate layer between impacts.

Jack Wolfe of the U.S. Geological Survey has gone even further. He has found what he thinks are the fossil remains of a lily pond from the very end of the Cretaceous. He reads a very detailed story from the fossils and tektites in the rocks. It started with the Chicxulub impact, which he puts in early June, causing an impact winter that froze the pond for a few weeks. The world thawed and started to recover. Then, ten to sixteen weeks after the first impact, a smaller object hit Manson, scattering more tiny tektites across the land, but not causing as much cooling.

Most geologists doubt that Wolfe can read so many details from rocks that formed 65 million years ago. However some suspect that at least two objects hit the earth at the end of the Cretaceous. The combination would have been worse than any single impact. Imagine what would happen to a devastated world, trying to recover from a giant impact, if it was hit by another object. The weakened survivors might not last through the second impact, even if that smaller impact normally would not have harmed them.

What kind of cosmic bad luck could have put two impacts so close together? It may not be as rare as you would think. In 1989 astronomers used powerful radar beams to get their first close look at an asteroid passing near the earth. They were startled to find that it was really two big rocks, held together by gravity. In 1992 they got an even better look at a second near-earth asteroid, and found it was also double! Scientists have found a few double craters on the Earth—what you would expect if a double asteroid hit. Other things also are possible. Shoemaker thinks a huge comet passing near the sun might have broken into two or more large chunks traveling on paths that crossed Earth's orbit. Others think the earth got in the way of a shower of comets.

There could have been more than two impacts. All known craters are not well dated, and some craters probably remain hidden. Erosion and plate motion have erased all traces of most ancient craters; they may have destroyed some recent ones as well. The great crater hunt is not over.

Guilty or Not?

The search for the cause of the Cretaceous extinctions also is not over. Most geologists now believe that an impact ended the Cretaceous, but the details are not certain. Chicxulub looks like the "smoking cannon," but no one has *proved* it. The dates are known only within a few hundred thousand years, which is good by geologic standards, but not a precise match. The relationship of Chicxulub and Manson remains a mystery.

Remember, too, that we also do not know many details of the extinctions. We are not sure about how fast the dinosaurs died, and we know nothing about the deaths of the pterosaurs and marine reptiles. An impact "certainly didn't do the dinosaurs any good," says David Archibald of San Diego State University. It may have killed the last of them. But he thinks they were fading long before the asteroid hit.

An impact is a dramatic event, and it is easy to call it *the* cause of the Cretaceous extinctions. Yet we are far from proving it was the *only* cause. The asteroid struck when the earth was changing. Life was changing as well at the end of the Cretaceous. The ammonoids had retreated to deep water. Small pterosaurs seem to have vanished, leaving only giants. The evidence seems to show that some animals were fading away before the impact.

Whatever happened was complex, and we have only a tiny bit of the evidence. Perhaps the impact finished off the last of a doomed and dying breed. Perhaps the dinosaurs were ailing, but could have recovered if the impact had not come at a bad time. Or perhaps the dinosaurs were doing fine until a disastrous impact turned out the lights. We know even less about other extinctions and about what happened in many other parts of the globe.

We may have enough evidence to make asteroid impact the leading suspect in the death of the dinosaurs and other victims of the Cretaceous mass extinctions. However we still are far from having enough evidence to prove the asteroid guilty "beyond a reasonable doubt."

We will see that this is much more than we know about other mass extinctions. Plenty of mysteries remain to be solved.

9

The Greatest Dying: The Permo-Triassic Extinctions

Both the Paleozoic and Mesozoic eras ended with mass extinctions. The one that ended the Mesozoic 65 million years ago, wiping out the dinosaurs, is better known, but the extinction that ended the Paleozoic 245 million years ago is the largest on record. Some geologists call it the time when the earth almost died.

The great Permo-Triassic dying gets its name because it came between the Permian period at the end of the Paleozoic and the Triassic period at the start of the Mesozoic. Scientists still argue about the death toll, but it was huge. Between 75 percent and 96 percent of animal species in the sea went extinct, more than at the end of the Cretaceous. Fewer species may have died on land, but time has clouded the patterns of the great Permian dying, which is three and a half times further in the past. The extinctions helped set the stage for the dinosaur age, just as the Cretaceous catastrophe set the stage for the mammals.

Like most other geological boundaries, the line between the Permian and Triassic is not obvious. I walked across it one day in a canyon in Capitol Reef National Park in Utah. A casual hiker might have missed it, but I was with students guided by a geology professor, Joanne Bourgeois. As we walked down the canyon from the grainy, red Triassic shales

The Permo-Triassic boundary at Capital Reef National Park in Utah. The light rocks are Permian limestone, the darker rocks are Triassic shale.

onto harder, paler Permian limestone, she told us we were crossing the greatest extinction of all time.

The actual boundary was missing, as it is in most places around the world. Sea level dropped near the end of the Permian, exposing the beds of the shallow sea that had covered Utah. Erosion washed away the last rocks formed in the Permian before sea level rose again in the Triassic. Then reddish sand washed into the new shallow waters, burying the Permian rocks for 245 million years.

A Dramatic Change

The small change in the rocks hides a big change in life between the Permian and the Triassic periods, both on land and in the sea, summarized in Table 2. Many big, awkward amphibians lived in the Permian period, although at first glance they might have looked like the bulky, short-legged reptiles which were becoming common. Some early reptiles had bony fins or sails standing up from their backs. Others were the distant ancestors of modern mammals. Life was a long way from the dinosaur age.

Many strange old animals vanished before the Permian ended, but the mass extinction claimed many others. Only a few survived into the Triassic. About half the species of land animals died at the end of the Permian, with the smaller the most likely to survive. The extinction took a heavy toll on reptiles built somewhat like mammals; one group of them later evolved into mammals, but most others died out during the dinosaur era. After the extinction, reptiles evolved into new forms: dinosaurs, mammals, pterosaurs, and large marine reptiles. The change was not rapid everywhere. Fossils from the Karroo Desert of South Africa show only a gradual change across the Permo-Triassic boundary, but that was an exception.

Land plants, too, changed at the end of the Permian period, although the change was slower than for animals. Trees with scaly bark, whose only living relatives are the tiny ground pines, faded away. So did other trees, related to small modern plants called horsetails. In their place grew conifers, like pines and firs, and cycads, which look like short, stubby palm trees and today live only in the tropics.

A Sea Change

The change on the ocean floor was much more dramatic than on land. For over 100 million years, many small animals had spent their lives fixed on the shallow seabed, feeding on tiny plants and animals floating in the water. They had evolved shells to protect themselves from predators and ocean currents and had formed communities in shallow Permian seas. Relatives of starfish called crinoids, or sea lilies, lived on stalks up to 20 inches (½ meter) long. Tiny creatures called bryozoans built lacy shell lattices above the ocean floor, while corals built massive reefs. Clams and brachiopods—very different animals with similar-looking shells—lived on the ocean floor. All the shells built thick layers of limestone and fossils during the Permian.

The Permo-Triassic extinctions changed the ocean floor forever, leaving few fixed animals. The great dying wiped out most brachiopods, crinoids, corals, and bryozoans; only the corals ever became common again. It wiped out all single-celled animals called fusulinids, about the size of grains of rice, which were so common in the Permian that their shells formed thick beds of limestone. Only the clams prospered, partly by digging into the muck at the ocean bottom.

Many creatures that swam or floated also died out. Slow-moving starfish and sea urchins suffered heavily. The last trilobites vanished, more than a quarter billion years after the first evolved. Some sharks went extinct, but most fish became much more common in the Triassic. Speed may have been their advantage.

Small differences between animals made big differences in survival.

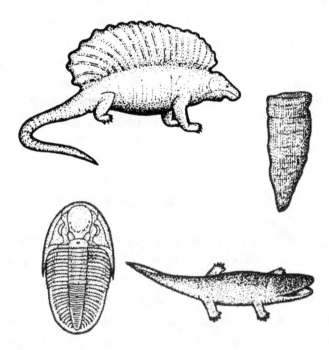

Victims of the Permian extinction included fin-backed reptiles, corals, large amphibians, and the last trilobites. (Adapted from *Extinctions* by Steven Stanely, © 1987 by Scientific American Books. Reprinted by Permission.)

The most vivid examples are the ammonoids and nautiloids, relatives of the octopus and squid, which lived in coiled shells. Like their modern relatives, they were predators who moved by squirting jets of water. The most obvious difference between them is that nautiloids have flat walls between shell chambers, while ammonoids have complexly curved walls. That gives no clue, however, to why the Permian extinctions almost wiped out the ammonoids but did little damage to the nautiloids.

Peter Ward, a specialist in ammonoids, says the crucial difference was in reproduction. Nautiloids produce only a few large young, which live in deep water. Ammonoids produced many tiny young, which lived near the ocean surface. Changes to the upper ocean could have wiped out young ammonoids without affecting young nautiloids in deeper water. Surviving nautiloids may have reproduced too slowly to spread rapidly in the empty Triassic ocean. On the other hand, the few surviving ammonoids reproduced quickly and soon spread through the early Triassic oceans. Later extinctions also hit ammonoids harder, and the Cretaceous extinctions wiped them out completely. The chambered nautilus survives today in the tropical Pacific.

The Permian World

The map of the Permian earth looks as alien as the creatures that inhabited it. A vast continent stretched almost from pole to pole, including all modern continents except part of Asia. This supercontinent, called Pangaea for "world-continent," was about 50 million years old then. It lasted for another 75 million years, until plate motion began tearing it apart. The center of Permian Pangaea may have had a harsh climate, with scorching summers and frigid winters, like modern central Asia. Ice sheets covered the South Pole early in the Permian, but we have no evidence of an ice age at the end. While the climate may have been harsh in some areas, it is hard to see how that alone could cause extinctions.

Sea level dropped dramatically near the end of the Permian. It fell slowly at first, then rapidly, to over 660 feet (200 meters) below the mid-Permian level. That is the largest drop known in the geological record, double the rise in sea level from the end of the Ice Age to the present. Then, strangely, sea level rose back in another couple of million years. No one knows why. Some scientists think a new ocean basin may have opened and swallowed the water temporarily; others think Pangaea may have risen in altitude. Some suspect the planet may have cooled enough to form large ice sheets for a few million years—although good evidence of ice is missing.

The fall in sea level drained large shallow seas, which had covered 40 percent of the continents. When the water was at its lowest it covered only about 10 percent of the continents, probably the least in the last 500 million years. (About 15 percent are covered by water today.) The retreat of the water surely didn't do any good to the animals that lived there. It also stopped rock formation in those areas, making it hard for geologists to find places where rocks record the whole sequence of events from the Permian to the Triassic. That may sound as if the drop in sea level was to blame, but recent ice ages have caused rapid rises and falls in sea level without mass extinctions in the seas.

The Permian map shows a few patterns of extinctions. Many victims had lived only in the tropical Tethys Sea before the great dying. Perhaps they had retreated to the warmest place left when the climate cooled. Or perhaps something happened in the tropics to cause the extinctions. Another pattern is that extinctions on land seem least severe in southern Pangaea, a huge land mass made up of what is now South America, Africa, India, Antarctica, and Australia. Were there fewer extinctions because those regions were farthest from the sea? It's hard to tell, because the little evidence we have shows few patterns, and land fossils from this period are rare.

Questions of Timing

Timing is one of the many uncertainties about an event—or maybe a series of events—that took place 245 million years ago. The Permian dying probably took longer than the Cretaceous extinctions. Doug Erwin, an expert at the Smithsonian Museum of Natural History, thinks the extinctions took about three million years; other estimates are between a few hundred thousand years and several million. Rocks that record the whole sequence of events at the end of the Permian would help resolve the question, but the drop in sea level makes them very rare.

In fact, geologists are not sure if all rocks they think come from the Permo-Triassic boundary are exactly the same age. Excess iridium is a handy marker that helps geologists match rocks formed at the end of the Cretaceous from around the world. With no such marker at the end of the Permian, geologists must define the boundary by fossils, usually ammonoids. The problem is that the same fossils aren't found everywhere. Different species lived in warm tropical waters and in cooler waters closer to the poles. Marine animals left no fossils on land, so scientists cannot use the same "clock" for land fossils, and the boundaries for land and sea may not date from the same time.

The last fossils of some animals come well before the end of the Permian. Does this mean they died out before the boundary? Or does it mean that we have yet to find the last fossils—like Peter Ward's discovery of the last ammonoids from the very end of the Cretaceous? We don't know.

Aftermath of the Extinctions

The seas were quiet after the great dying. The dull gray shales and siltstones that formed in the oceans at the start of the Triassic contain very few fossils. It looks like the aftermath of a massacre. Just a few creatures were left alive on the ocean floor.

Some animals took advantage of the empty world. Bursts of evolution often follow mass extinctions, with survivors adapting rapidly to occupy the places left by the extinct. The few surviving ammonoids evolved rapidly in the early Triassic and soon spread through the seas, but the ocean bottom remained almost empty long after the Permian extinctions. More than 10 million years later, only a scattering of clams and snails lived on the ocean bottom. It was even longer before the return of reefs and the many creatures that lived on them.

At the very start of the Triassic, a bulky, hog-sized plant eater called Lystrosaurus became so common on land that it left most of the fossils found in some places. However, other reptiles evolved rapidly into new forms. The Triassic really belonged to the thecodonts, graceful, lightly built reptiles with long tails, which ran on two large rear legs and were ancestors of the dinosaurs. The first thecodonts appeared in the Permian and spread rapidly after they survived the mass extinction. Other Triassic reptiles evolved into the flying pterosaurs and the giant marine reptiles. Dinosaurs evolved later, but had spread over the whole world by the late Triassic.

Some puzzling things happened as the world recovered from the Permian extinctions. Many common snails disappeared in the late Permian, then reappeared more than 25 million years later in the middle Triassic. Scientists do not think they returned from the dead; the snails just left no fossils we have yet found. But does that mean they were very rare, or that they were common in places where fossils were not preserved?

Seeking a Cause

The Permian extinctions remain much more a mystery than those at the end of the Cretaceous. Some clues are intriguing. Why did ammonoids react so differently from nautiloids? Why was the ocean floor so barren for so long after the extinction? Why did a single plant-eating animal become so common at the start of the Triassic?

It is tempting to suspect a catastrophe. After the Alvarezes found excess iridium at the end of the Cretaceous, other geologists searched for it at the end of the Permian. Although a couple of scientists claim to have found a little extra iridium, most agree there is no sign of the sharp increase in iridium caused by an asteroid impact.

Could a low-iridium comet have hit the earth instead? A big enough block of ice could have done a lot of damage, but a comet impact would have produced shocked quartz and a crater. Long and careful searches have found no sign of either at the end of the Permian. Perhaps something hit the vast world-ocean, Panthallassa, that surrounded Pangaea.

Victims (total extinction)

SEA

Trilobites—in decline before end of Permian
Rugose corals—fixed on ocean floor, only in tropics
Fusulinids—lived on ocean floor, only in tropics

Barely survived

SEA

Ammonoids—marine swimmers (recovered quickly)
Other corals—fixed on ocean floor
Brachiopods—mostly fixed on ocean floor
Bryozoans—fixed on ocean floor, tropical
Sea urchins—slow-moving, ocean-floor dwellers
Starfish—slow-moving, ocean-floor dwellers
Crinoids (sea lilies)—fixed to ocean floor

LAND

Amphibians
Mammal-like reptiles

Minor damage

SEA

Bivalves (clams, mussels)—lived in bottom mud
Snails—mobile ocean-floor dwellers
Sharks—swimmers

Little or no damage

SEA

Nautiloids—swimmers
Fish—swimmers

TABLE 2 *Permo-Triassic Victims and Survivors.*

The shifting of continental plates has destroyed all the crust of that ancient ocean. However, no one has found any solid evidence for such an impact, and it does not match other evidence, like the slow speed of the extinctions.

What about volcanic eruptions? One reason Officer and Drake suggested volcanoes killed the dinosaurs was that other gigantic eruptions matched other mass extinctions. The greatest eruptions of all were in Siberia, very close to the end of the Permian. In 600,000 years—maybe less—they poured out some half a million cubic miles (2 million cubic kilometers) of lava, forming deposits called the Siberian Traps, which cover an area almost the size of Alaska. Could the eruption of close to a cubic mile of lava a year have generated enough volcanic gases to disrupt climate? A dramatic cooling could have caused ice sheets to form, which would have taken water from the oceans and caused sea level to drop. It's an interesting idea, but direct evidence is missing. Perhaps the eruptions affected sea level in some other way. If the ocean basins had expanded or the continents had risen, sea level would have seemed to drop.

The dramatic change in sea level looks suspicious, whatever its cause. Some evidence seems to fit. Creatures that lived in fixed spots on the bottom of shallow seas suffered the most. Their living space shrank as sea level dropped, and they couldn't migrate easily. Fewer animals went extinct in central Pangaea. Could that be because they were far from the sea? The problem is that other dramatic changes in sea level did not cause mass extinctions in the seas; and even if varying sea level caused the extinctions, we don't know what made the water fall and rise.

Climate change is always a suspect, but scientists don't agree on what type. Some suggest the world may have slipped into an ice age—but again, we have no evidence of huge ice sheets at the end of the Permian. Others suggest that sediments exposed on dry ocean floors may have taken oxygen from the air and added carbon dioxide, perhaps starving the seas of the oxygen that animals needed. But those are only suggestions. The Permo-Triassic extinctions are a mystery yet to be solved.

10

The Triassic Extinctions

New animals spread across the land and sea in the Triassic period that followed the Permian extinctions. The Triassic was part of the Mesozoic era of middle life, which we call the age of dinosaurs. Yet other reptiles dominated the land for most of the Triassic. The oldest dinosaur fossils date from 230 million years ago. Dinosaur fossils do not become common until the late Triassic. The most familiar dinosaurs evolved after the Triassic—the giant sauropods, the terrifying carnosaurs, the duck-billed hadrosaurs, and the tank-like ceratopsians, ankylosaurs, and stegosaurs. Pick up any dinosaur book, and you will be surprised how few animals shown lived in the Triassic period.

The Triassic was a time of change, partway between the ancient life of clumsy amphibians and the middle life of the dinosaurs. Reptiles evolved into many forms. The extinct dinosaurs, pterosaurs, ichthyosaurs, and plesiosaurs, and the living crocodiles, turtles, and mammals all appeared for the first time in the Triassic. Yet it was also one of the shortest distinct groupings of life known, according to paleontologist Peter Ward. A mass extinction ended the Triassic 202 million years ago, clearing the world for the dinosaurs and other animals of the Jurassic period that followed.

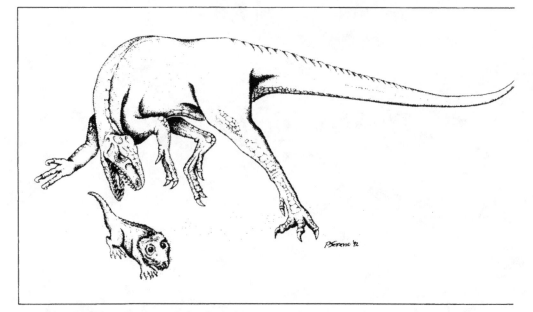

Dog-sized Eoraptor, one of the first dinosaurs, chases a mammal-like reptile 225 million years ago in Argentina. (Courtesy of Paul Sereno / University of Chicago)

Changes on the Land

Both the map of the world and its animal inhabitants were very different in the Triassic than today. Most land was part of Pangaea, the vast world-continent. Several groups of reptiles spread across the land after the Permian extinctions. The two most common were the mammal-like reptiles and the archosaurs—the dinosaurs and their kin.

Scientists classify the two types of reptiles by counting the holes in their skulls. Mammal-like reptiles and modern mammals have one opening on each side behind the eye. Archosaurs have two holes on each side. It's not a difference you notice in live animals, but it helps in sorting fossils.

If you had looked at living animals, you would have seen many other differences. The first archosaurs were thecodonts, small meat eaters with bodies like lizards and long, thick tails. They stood upright and ran on two long rear legs set under their bodies. They could run much faster than older reptiles and amphibians with sprawling legs. Some thecodonts soon evolved into dinosaurs and crocodiles (although early crocodiles had long legs). Look carefully at skeletons of dinosaurs, even the bulky brontosaurus, and you can see that their rear legs are longer than the front ones.

Mammal-like reptiles stayed on four legs. Although we think of mammals as lighter than dinosaurs, early mammal-like reptiles were bulkier and heavier than early archosaurs, with thicker legs and shorter, fatter tails. One group of meat eaters called cynodonts included small animals that evolved into the first mammals during the Triassic. Those early mammals stayed small, about the size of mice, and that probably helped them survive the mass extinction at the end of the Triassic.

The Triassic extinction wiped out many larger land animals including thecodonts, many mammal-like reptiles, and some large amphibians. The dinosaurs were among the survivors that benefited from the ex-

Lystrosaurus (left) *watches other mammal-like reptiles.* (Courtesy of Doubleday, from C. L. Fenton, M. A. Fenton, P. V. Rich, and T. H. Rich, *The Fossil Book*)

tinction. The largest Triassic dinosaurs stood 20 feet (6 meters) high and shared the world with many other animals. In the Jurassic period that followed, dinosaurs spread widely and evolved into many new forms, including giants weighing over 50 tons (45,000 kilograms) and stretching up to 100 feet (30 meters) long. Their cousins the crocodiles also survived. So did the pterosaurs, turtles, and lizards, which evolved from other Triassic reptiles.

Nature kindly collected samples of life on land at the end of the Triassic in the bottoms of several long, narrow lakes in the part of Pangaea that became the east coast of North America. The reddish brown rocks lie along the Connecticut River valley in New England, in northern New Jersey, and in Pennsylvania, Virginia, and North Carolina. The best animal fossils from the very end of the Triassic are in Nova Scotia. Paul Olsen of the Lamont-Doherty Geological Observatory in Palisades, New York, says those fossils show that the extinctions took less than a million years. At first only a few animals appeared to replace the old Triassic species.

Old lake deposits from New Jersey and Virginia hold important clues about plants at the end of the Triassic. Sarah Fowell of Lamont-Doherty found a layer in which up to 90 percent of the fossil spores come from ferns. It sits on top of rocks containing the usual Triassic plant fossils and spores, and just under rocks containing the first Jurassic plant fossils. It looks as if a disaster stopped the growth of Triassic plants and cleared the land, so ferns could sprout. Then survivors of the disaster reappeared and evolved into other forms in the Jurassic. Other scientists have seen a similar pattern in rocks formed on land at the time of the Cretaceous extinctions.

Extinctions in the Water

The extinctions at the end of the Triassic also changed life in the seas. Ichthyosaurs survived, but two other types of Triassic marine reptiles did not—nothosaurs and placodonts. The placodonts were thick-bodied animals with flippers or paddles like modern seals or walruses. Massive bony plates in their mouths let them crush shells so that they could eat the shelled animals common in Triassic oceans. The nothosaurs were long and thin, part otter and part lizard, with short legs and a long neck. Some evolved into the long-necked plesiosaurs, the sea serpents of later dinosaur times, but the rest vanished. It is not clear why some marine reptiles survived and others did not—or even if the victims died during or before the Triassic extinction.

Fish evolved rapidly in the Triassic, with many new families appearing. Some were very successful, including the first of the teleost fish that dominate modern lakes, rivers, and oceans. While the new families survived the Triassic extinction well, older types, like relatives of the sturgeon and paddlefish, suffered heavily.

As for other extinctions the best fossil evidence comes from hard-shelled animals that left their hard parts scattered over the sea floor. The death toll did not match that at the end of the Permian, but it was still large.

Survivors of the Permian extinction filled Triassic oceans with a mixture of old and new animals. The few ammonoid species that survived the Permian extinction proliferated to yield thousands of species by the late Triassic. They shared the seas with their nautiloid cousins and with belemnoids—shell-less relatives with internal bullet-shaped counter-weights several centimeters long that readily survive as fossils. Brachiopods had returned to the ocean floor, but they shared Triassic waters with the relatives of modern clams, which had been rare before the Permian extinction. Eel-like conodont animals left behind their hard teeth, which geologists have long used as a fossil clock to date rocks. Modern corals, called hexacorals, started to form reefs, which grew large by the late Triassic.

The Triassic extinction wiped out only one group—the conodonts—but it did great damage to many others. Of the thousands of ammonoid species, no more than three survived. Some nautiloid species also went extinct. Many species of both clams and brachiopods vanished. British geologist Anthony Hallam says that 92 percent of the clam species in Europe did not survive the end of the Triassic, although some may have survived elsewhere. Snails also suffered major extinctions. Corals survived, but for a time stopped forming reefs in the shallow tropical waters covering Europe.

The groups that did survive the Triassic extinctions soon recovered. By the middle Jurassic, the seas were once again full of ammonoids, clams, and brachiopods, although the brachiopods were slowly declining. Corals were again forming vast reefs beneath the waves—reefs larger than previous ones. New marine reptiles were eating the shelly survivors.

What Ended the Triassic?

Many geologists believe that the Triassic mass extinctions took place at the same time on land and in the oceans, but this is hard to prove. One problem is that geologists use fossil ammonoids, which were not present on land, to set the time scale in rocks from the ocean. Another is that scientists have found few rock formations that span the end of the Triassic and the start of the Jurassic without interruption.

The picture is complicated because geologists have found signs of another, smaller extinction at least several million years—and perhaps up to 20 million years—before the end of the Triassic. Fossils are scarce between the two extinctions. That makes it hard to be sure whether some animals vanished in the first extinction, the second, or sometime in between.

Scientists have collected some evidence about what happened at the end of the Triassic, which we can compare to our suspect list. The speed of the extinction tells us we should look for evidence of an impact. However, rocks from the Triassic-Jurassic boundary show no signs of excess iridium, which would come from an asteroid impact like the one at the end of the Cretaceous. Nor do they show chemical or isotopic evidence of anything strange.

Some scientists think there may have been an impact at the end of the Triassic—but by a low-iridium comet rather than a high-iridium asteroid. Evidence for such an impact comes from rocks formed in a shallow sea covering part of Italy. David M. Bice of Carleton College in Minnesota found tiny quartz crystals with flaws produced by shock waves—the fingerprint of an impact—in rocks formed at the very end of the Triassic. Cathryn Newton of Syracuse University, who worked with him, found fossils of Triassic animals in the layers below the thin layer of shale that contained shocked quartz. The rocks above that layer contained few fossils, as if few animals lived in the ocean after the event that left the shocked quartz. There was no excess iridium anywhere.

Most geologists consider shocked quartz to be good evidence of an impact. If a large comet hit the earth, the impact would throw countless tiny shocked quartz grains into the atmosphere, which would drift to the ground slowly. A big comet impact could do plenty of damage without scattering iridium all over the planet. However, the picture is complicated. Bice found shocked quartz in two other shale layers. Could that mean that two other impacts came shortly before the boundary impact? Or did something concentrate shocked quartz in just those three layers of shale, avoiding the surrounding limestone? We don't know.

Other scientists have looked for shocked quartz at the end of the Triassic, but only one Russian researcher has reported finding any. That may mean that the others didn't look hard enough, that they didn't look at the right boundary layer, or that the tiny grains were lost or destroyed. Or it may mean that something other than a big impact produced the shocked quartz that Bice found. One possibility is a smaller impact nearby, like the one that formed the .8-mile (1.2-kilometer) Barringer Meteor Crater in Arizona.

For a while before Bice's discovery, scientists thought they had a good candidate for an impact at the end of the Triassic period. The 40-mile (70-kilometer) crater that holds Lake Manicouagan about 300 miles (500 kilometers) north of the Maine border in Quebec seemed to be about the right age. However, while Bice peered through a microscope at quartz grains, two Canadian scientists were carefully dating rocks from Manicouagan. They found that the crater formed 214 million years ago— but that the layers that mark the end of the Triassic in Nova Scotia were formed 202 million years ago. Unless the dates are wrong, that 12-

million-year difference means the Manicouagan is innocent of causing the extinctions at the end of the Triassic.

If not Manicouagan, where could an impact have taken place? The ocean floor is a good possibility. It covers two-thirds of the earth's surface, so two-thirds of impacts should be in the water. In addition, subduction eventually destroys ocean crust by pulling it back into the earth's mantle. The oldest known ocean crust is about 180 million years old. All the ocean floor that existed 200 million years ago has been destroyed, except for a few small pieces that have been pasted onto the sides of the continents. If a big comet formed a crater in the ocean floor 200 million years ago, it no longer exists.

We could also have missed a crater on the continents. It took years of research to recognize the Chicxulub Crater along the Mexican coast because it was buried by thick layers of limestone formed when shallow oceans covered the area. Older craters could be buried more deeply or might have eroded away if the land was exposed.

Other Possibilities

The grains of shocked quartz in the Italian rocks are not the only smudged fingerprints left at the scene of the Triassic extinctions. Geologists have evidence of other things that might have caused some extinctions.

One is the start of the breakup of Pangaea. About 200 million years ago, cracks were appearing in the world-continent. They began as narrow rifts, which filled with water, forming long, narrow lakes. Some of those lakes filled with sand and debris, forming the fossil-rich red rocks of Connecticut, New Jersey, and Nova Scotia. A few similar lakes exist today, including Lake Tanganyika in Africa and Lake Baikal in Siberia. Millions of years later, some cracks opened further, tearing Pangaea apart. In time the cracks grew into the Atlantic and Indian oceans. Was it just a coincidence that the first cracks started opening at a time of mass extinctions? We don't know.

Another geological clue is a change in how fast limestone formed in tropical oceans at the end of the Triassic. Limestone is made mostly of shells of things that live in the sea. Animals and some tiny plants collect calcium carbonate from ocean water to build their shells. When they die, the shells settle to the bottom, usually in pieces. Over many years, the shelly debris piles up, and in time becomes limestone. Limestone forms faster in warm water than in cool water. At the end of the Triassic, limestone formation slowed down. That might mean that the temperatures cooled, causing extinctions.

It is hard to tell how much climate affected the extinctions because some critical evidence is missing from the end of the Triassic. We think the climate was warmer than today, but probably not as warm as it was toward the end of the dinosaur era in the Cretaceous.

Sea level also is important. A sharp rise or fall in sea level might kill many species that live in shallow water or along the coast, by exposing them, drowning them, or taking away the places they live. However, geologists are not sure if the sea level was rising, falling, or about constant at the end of the Triassic. That may mean sea level was not changing as fast or as much as it did at the end of the Permian—or it may mean that the change was too fast to leave clear evidence in the rocks.

We are left with a mystery. Changes in climate or sea level could account for some extinctions. A large object from space may have hit the earth. Maybe different things caused different extinctions. Or perhaps the extinctions were spread out over more time in the late Triassic than we think. Many more years of research remain before the mystery can be solved.

11

Other Mass Extinctions

So far, we have talked about three mass extinctions, but they are not the whole story. Evidence for others goes back more than half a billion years. The very first animals that left small hard shells may have been victims of a mass extinction. The trilobites after them also suffered mass extinctions. So did many other living things, from tiny one-celled plants and animals to giant dinosaurs and large mammals.

The Permian, Triassic, and Cretaceous extinctions are three of what some geologists call the big five of all time (marked with heavy arrows in Table 1). The other two came during the Paleozoic era of early life. One ended the Ordovician period, 438 million years ago; the other came about 367 million years ago in the late Devonian. Both extinctions changed the world, but their victims were not as famous as the dinosaurs. Some geologists think a sixth extinction, which wiped out the first small shelly animals more than half a billion years ago, belongs on that list of great dyings.

As we saw in chapter 5, scientists look for peaks in the curve showing extinctions over time. The big five (or six) are the largest peaks. We also see smaller peaks, which seem to tell of smaller extinctions. Trilobites suffered a few during the Cambrian. Dinosaurs and marine reptiles suffered one at the end of the Jurassic period, about 144 million years ago. Mammals and some shelled ocean animals suffered another at the end of the Eocene period, about 37 million years ago. Some smaller peaks may not really show great dyings, but only times when scientists misread the fossil record, seeing too many extinctions. Still, studying these times may yield clues about mass extinctions.

Early Extinctions

We have not yet found fossil records of mass extinctions before animals evolved hard shells, but they must have occurred. The spread of oxygen in the atmosphere about two billion years ago must have wiped out many species that could not live in an oxygen atmosphere, but those tiny, single-celled organisms left few fossils. Many-celled animals with soft bodies evolved much later, about 600 million years ago. These animals, called the Ediacara fauna, after the place where they were discovered in Australia, look very different from the animals that lived in the Cambrian period that followed. We don't know if they evolved into other forms or vanished suddenly.

The first good evidence of a mass extinction—which may have been very severe—comes in the early Cambrian, 530 to 520 million years ago. The victims were small shelly animals, which left the first common fossils; sponge-like animals with hard conical shells called archaeocyathids; and trilobites. New trilobites soon replaced the old ones, but the small shelly animals and archaeocyathids did not recover.

Three extinctions of North American trilobites in the late Cambrian have been better studied by geologists. Warm tropical seas covered most of the continent, which at the time lay on the equator. Three times over a period of several million years, new trilobites appeared and spread rapidly across the continent, then most of them vanished. A few other sea animals were affected, but most victims were trilobites. Although trilobites recovered each time, they had to share the ocean floor with other new animals.

Trilobites shed their old shells as they outgrew them, so one animal could leave many fossils. Their many fossils give scientists plenty of data to study. The fossils show that three times, 40 percent to 90 percent of trilobite species vanished quickly, probably in under a thousand years. They seem to have vanished at the same time in all of North America.

What killed the trilobites? No one has found iridium or shocked quartz, the fingerprints of an impact. Steven M. Stanley of Johns Hopkins University thinks the ocean got too cold each time. The new trilobites always came from deeper, cooler water. The cool-water trilobites then adapted to the warmer, shallow waters and evolved into many new species—which were wiped out by the next cold spell. While that is the best idea so far, it leaves many questions open. The change in trilobites is the main evidence that temperature changed, but it could mean something else. Maybe the cold-water trilobites arrived only after something else killed their warm-water cousins. And if the water did grow colder, we do not know why.

The End of the Ordovician

Many more animals had evolved shells by the time of the first of the big-five mass extinctions that ended the Ordovician period 438 million years ago. Nautiloids pushed their cone-shaped shells by expelling jets of water, making them the most deadly predators of Ordovician seas. The first corals evolved and grew reefs. Bryozoans grew lacy shells on the sea floor; graptolites grew stick-like shells that let them float in the water. Brachiopods prospered; their shells are the most common Ordovician fossils. Then something happened. Many brachiopods, graptolites, trilobites, bryozoans, nautiloids, conodont animals, and reef builders vanished. No entire groups went extinct, but all were affected.

What happened? The leading suspect is a drop in temperature. Graptolite fossils give good clues, because they lived in different climate zones. Some types lived near the equator, others lived in the temperate zone, and still others lived in cooler waters. As time passed in the Ordovician, cool-water graptolites moved closer to the equator. So did cool-water brachiopods. The animals seem to have come toward the equator along with cooler waters.

The late Ordovician world, before the extinctions. The many-armed conical animals are nautiloids. (Courtesy of Field Museum of Natural History, Chicago [Neg. #GEO80820])

More evidence of cooling comes from an unlikely place—the Sahara Desert. That region was near the South Pole in the late Ordovician, when glaciers started to grow. Rocks in the Sahara show the scars of thick Ordovician ice sheets. As the ice grew, it took water from the oceans, and water levels dropped. The cold and lower sea level may have been deadly to animals that evolved during warmer times; their cold-water cousins survived to inherit the world.

The evidence adds up to the best case for climate change as a cause of extinctions. There is no sign of an impact or other catastrophe. However, the evidence still is not strong enough to prove that climate change caused the extinctions.

Late Devonian Extinctions

The fifth of the big extinctions came about 367 million years ago, several million years before the end of the Devonian period. Plants and insects had begun to live on land. Their fossils show no signs of a mass extinction, but that could be because their fossils are rare. It was life in the water that suffered.

Many animals that were hard hit in the Ordovician also suffered in the Devonian extinction. Reefs, which had recovered after the Ordovician extinction, vanished for a while after the Devonian extinction. Many brachiopods, conodont animals, and trilobites went extinct. So did many other shelled animals, including ammonoids, which had evolved from the nautiloids.

The Devonian extinction also wiped out many fish with bodies covered with bony plates instead of scales. These strange armored fish, called placodonts, were the first to evolve jaws, which made them deadly predators. Their armor protected them, probably from other fish. They became common in the mid-Devonian, but many species died in the great extinction. The rest were gone by about 350 million years ago, leaving the water open for modern fish, which rely on speed rather than armor to escape their enemies.

Geologists have different ideas about how long the extinctions took. Charles A. Sandberg of the U.S. Geological Survey in Denver says rocks in Germany show that sea level rose and fell in the course of 100,000 years, and the extinctions happened in a time from days to 20,000 years. Other scientists think they took at least a million years.

A few scientists have found clues of a possible impact near the time of the extinction. Chinese scientists have found a layer that contains tiny tektites and about ten times more iridium than normal, as well as what may be a tsunami deposit. Carbon isotopes also indicate that the number of living things may have dropped. Scientists in Belgium have found tiny tektites close to the extinction boundary.

Others have serious doubts. They say something else could have concentrated iridium, that the tektites don't occur in the boundary layer, and that any impacts might have been too small to cause extinctions. They also note that other rocks from the same time do not show impact fingerprints. However, 367 million years could have destroyed tektites and blurred other impact fingerprints.

An impact is not the only possibility. The growth of glaciers on the southern continents after the extinction is evidence of changing climate that might have affected ocean life. Some scientists think the ocean water changed; stagnant water containing little oxygen might have flowed into shallow seas, choking animals. The jury is still out; more evidence is needed before a verdict can be delivered.

Smaller Extinctions

Scientists who study the history of life also have found other times when the rate of extinction was much larger than normal, but not as high as during the big-five mass extinctions. They mark times of change on the planet. Most come at times where geologists draw lines between periods in the planet's history, but this is not an accident. Geologists drew those lines because they saw the changes, which we now recognize as extinctions.

The late Cambrian extinctions of trilobites mentioned earlier are among these smaller extinctions. Table 1 lists others, but that list is not complete. Scientists do not agree on how to count extinctions, or on what to consider a mass extinction. It may seem as if they have not agreed on the rules of the game, but it really means that they are looking at different parts of the problem—and getting different answers.

What really happens can be very complex and hard to understand. To see why, we can look at a couple of examples that have been studied carefully.

A Deadly Volcano

Some great catastrophes devastate large areas but do not cause global mass extinctions. A huge volcanic eruption near what is now the Carolina coast killed virtually everything in parts of eastern North America 454 million years ago, says Robert Sloan of the University of Minnesota. Volcanic ash formed thick layers in the shallow seas of eastern North America as far as 1,000 miles (1,600 kilometers) away in Minnesota. It was originally 14 feet (4.2 meters) thick in Virginia and 11 inches (27 centimeters) thick in Minnesota. The eruption scattered 200 to 800 cubic miles (1,000 to 4,000 cubic kilometers) of volcanic ash over North America and Europe when the continents were much closer.

The ash killed everything that had lived in the shallow seas where it fell. After it settled, animals from the south and west moved in to claim the empty space. Species that lived only in small areas were wiped out; Sloan says 90 percent of trilobite species went extinct. However, species spread over larger areas suffered only minor losses, like the conodont animals, only 10 percent of which died out.

When Continents Collide

Continental collisions also can kill off many species, but in a very different way. They put plants and animals that evolved in different places onto the same land mass. This forces them to compete with one another, and, as Darwin showed, the fittest will survive. We can see what happens if we look at the animals of North and South America, because the land bridge between the two, the Isthmus of Panama, formed only about three million years ago.

For most of the last 100 million years, South America was as isolated as Australia is today. Unusual animals can evolve on isolated land masses. Australia has koalas and kangaroos. South America had giant ground sloths, 10-foot (3-meter) tall meat-eating birds, and armadillos— including giants as well as the small modern type. Marsupial mammals like the kangaroo and opossum did almost as well in South America as in Australia.

North America, however, was linked to Asia and Europe many times over the last 100 million years. The link to Asia came when the shallow Bering Strait was dry land—as it was 12,000 to 15,000 years ago, when the first Native Americans crossed it from Asia. The link to Europe was across Greenland, before the North Atlantic opened. Because of those links, the animals of ancient North America were similar to those of Europe, Asia, and Africa.

Unusual animals evolved while South America was isolated from other continents. The large animals at left are Megatheriums, ground sloths almost as large as elephants. At right are glyptodonts, large relatives of the armadillo. (Courtesy of Field Museum of Natural History, Chicago [Neg. #CK73942])

After the land bridge was formed, animals moved both north and south across Panama. At first natives of each continent roamed the other, but slowly the North Americans crowded out most South Americans. North American carnivores spread south, while the giant predatory birds of South America vanished. North American camels and horses spread south, evolving into forms like the llama, a camel we consider a native of the south. South American plant eaters like the giant armadillos died out. Only three common North American mammals—armadillos, porcupines, and opossums—came from the south.

If we look back we can see what looks like a mass extinction of South American birds and mammals. We are close enough in time to see that the cause was the Panama land bridge, which brought animals from the north. However, if hundreds of millions of years had passed, plate motion could have erased evidence of the land bridge, and we might be puzzling over what would seem to be another mysterious mass extinction.

Hidden Extinctions

Detectives look for footprints and tire tracks on dirt, not on pavement. In the same way, scientists look for clues to mass extinctions in the fossils that are the easiest to find—hard-shelled animals that lived on the ocean floor.

The problem is that those animals are only a small fraction of all the creatures that ever lived. Insects are by far the most common animals on land today. They can leave fossils like the imprint I found not far from the Permo-Triassic boundary. Amber, the fossil sap of ancient trees, beautifully preserves some fossil insects. However, we don't know their fossil record well enough to tell if insects ever suffered mass extinctions.

Soft-bodied animals leave even fewer fossils, and their fate, too, is a big mystery. Scientists have found a few fossils showing strange early soft-bodied animals that lived a little over half a billion years ago. Many look very different than anything that lives today. Did they evolve into other forms? Or did they vanish completely? We don't know. We have only a few "snapshots" of these creatures, taken by accident when fine mud covered their bodies and preserved them. Their fate is another mystery.

12

Modern Extinctions

Mass extinctions are not as dead as the dinosaurs. Extinctions continue today, but they have nothing to do with asteroids or volcanoes. Their main cause is the billions of people who live on this planet. We are crowding out many other species.

You can see how much land we use if you fly across the United States. The neat patterns of farms cover the central third of the country, from Ohio to Colorado. Crops cover 21 percent of the United States. Another 26 percent is permanent pasture for animals. That means we farm almost half the country—and that counts Alaska and the mountains and deserts of the western states. Woodlands cover another 29 percent of the country, but most of those forests are cut regularly for lumber and paper. Only 4 percent of the United States consists of tracts of uninhabited land large enough (over 1,500 square miles or 4,000 square kilometers) to be called wilderness.

The world as a whole may seem wilder—39 percent of the world's land is wilderness. However, that covers large areas where people cannot live—deserts like the Sahara and Gobi, the frozen tundras of Siberia and northern Canada, and the ice sheets of Greenland and Antarctica. People use most land that can be farmed. Crops cover 68 percent of crowded Bangladesh, where, as in many other countries, there is no wil-

Wilderness (dark shading) *covers 39 percent of the continents, but most of that area is frozen tundra, desert, or glacial ice, which people have left alone because they don't want to live there.* (Based on 1988 data from the Sierra Club)

derness at all. Table 3 shows the divisions of land use around the globe.

Some plants and animals have learned to live with people. Our trees are full of gray squirrels; raccoons raid suburban garbage cans. Rats and mice are everywhere. Ragweed grows along roadsides. Pigeons and sea gulls scavenge in the cities and garbage dumps. Moose live in the paper-company woods of northern Maine.

However, a world crowded with people has little or no place for other animals. Giants like the elephant and rhinoceros need too much room and are threatened by poachers. Only 11,000 rhinos remain in the world. People have killed predators like wolves and tigers because they threaten livestock and don't make good neighbors. Other animals, like the California condor, have been harmed by pesticides, or simply crowded out of their habitat. As their numbers drop, these animals grow more vulnerable to extinction, a fate many have already met.

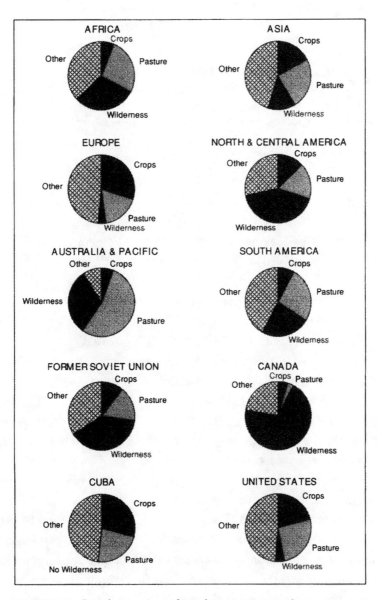

TABLE 3 *Land use in selected countries and continents. "Other" land includes cities, forests where lumber is cut, and small wild areas. "Wilderness" includes deserts, tundra, ice sheets, and other "wastelands." Arctic tundra and the Greenland ice sheet make up most wilderness in North and Central America. Many countries have no land that meets the standard definition of wilderness.*

Death at the End of the Ice Age

It does not take modern civilization to cause extinctions. Explorers wiped out many species on isolated islands from the 1500s to the 1800s. However, even Stone Age people may have wiped out many species— the giant mammals of the Ice Age.

The Ice Age was the time of giants in North America. Mastodons and mammoths, cousins of the elephant, had thick fur and skins that protected them from the cold. The giant Shasta ground sloth, about 10 feet (3 meters) long, roamed western forests. The giant beaver, as large as a black bear, gnawed on trees with front teeth several inches long. Fearsome predators roamed the land: saber-toothed tigers, the American lion, and bears and wolves larger than their modern cousins. Native horses and camels roamed the plains. (Modern horses were imported by European colonists in the last 500 years.)

Those animals were among the Ice Age *megafauna,* thirty-five to forty species of large animals that went extinct between about 12,000 and 9,000 years ago. The great ice sheets that had covered Canada and the northern states were melting after thousands of years. North America was warming; the western states were drying. Tundra was turning to forest, and forest to desert.

At the same time, Native Americans were spreading rapidly through the Americas. Early Native Americans were hunters, and must have killed some animals for food. They may have killed predators to protect themselves, just as later European settlers shot wolves prowling near their cabins. The early hunters may not have killed all the large animals, but they may have killed too many for the species to survive. The predators may have died after their prey were gone.

That suspicious timing is not proof of guilt. The ashes of ancient camp fires include bones of extinct mammoths, as well as those of bison, elk, and many other large animals that survive today. However, few signs of human activity have been found near remains of many other extinct animals. Some scientists think this means climate change had pushed the large animals near extinction before humans arrived.

Some evidence for that view comes from other continents, where the big animals did not vanish as soon as humans arrived. Humans lived in Europe long before they reached North America, but the big animals vanished about the same time on the two continents (although not as fast in Europe). That might point to loss of the ice, as would the survival of the elephant, rhinoceros, and hippopotamus in ice-free Africa, where humans evolved. The case is less clear in Australia, where extinctions occurred about 30,000 years ago, after humans arrived, but before the Ice Age stopped chilling the continent.

Other clues point to humans as the culprits. Over the past two million years, vast ice sheets have many times covered Canada and northern Europe, then melted back, only to return. Warm periods of about 10,000 years separate ice ages of 100,000 years. Earlier growth and retreat of the ice caused some extinctions, but never as many as the last one.

We may never know exactly what killed the megafauna. Human hunters probably contributed to their extinction, but climate change may already have reduced their numbers to dangerously low levels. Did it take the combination of climate change and hunting to kill them? Or was one or the other enough?

Dead as a Dodo

Humans have also wiped out many plants and animals that evolved on isolated islands. Island life is very vulnerable because numbers are small and animals have few defenses. The classic example is the dodo, which lived on the isolated island of Mauritius, 500 miles (800 kilometers) east of Madagascar in the Indian Ocean. The dodo evolved from birds that flew to the island long ago. With no predators on the island, dodos had lost both the ability to fly and their fear of large animals. They waddled awkwardly, weighed up to 50 pounds (23 kilograms) and were up to 40 inches (1 meter) tall.

In the 1600s, Mauritius became a common stopping point for ships crossing the Indian Ocean. After a bleak diet of salted and dried food, sailors would gladly eat any native wildlife they could find. Dodos reportedly smelled and tasted bad, but those sailors were hungry. The birds never learned to flee from humans. Their fate was sealed when people brought hogs and dogs to the island, which ate young dodos and their eggs. The last live dodo was seen in 1681.

The same has happened on many other islands. Early human settlers on Cyprus feasted on hog-sized pygmy hippos 10,500 years ago, wiping them out. Before humans settled New Zealand, about A.D. 1300, the largest animals were moas, flightless birds up to 8 feet (2.5 meters) tall. Their ancestors had flown to the islands and had the place to themselves. With no competition, they became the predominant plant eaters and did not have to be fast to run away from predators. They were easy prey for the human settlers, who killed them all within a few hundred years.

Madagascar once was the home of giant flightless birds called elephant

The first human settlers on Cyprus feasted on hog-sized pygmy hippos 10,500 years ago, leaving the thick layers of bone at the bottom—and wiping out the animals. (Courtesy of Rolfe Mandel / University of Nebraska at Omaha)

birds. They were 10 feet (3 meters) tall, weighed up to 1,000 pounds (450 kilograms), and laid 13-inch (33-centimeter) eggs. They may have inspired tales of the legendary roc, which supposedly could carry elephants off in its claws. However, early human settlers wiped them out.

Domestic animals have added to the damage caused by humans. Sheep and goats eat island plants, while cats, dogs, and rats kill island wildlife. Thick forests covered the South Atlantic island of Saint Helena when Portuguese sailors discovered it in 1501. Goats arrived a dozen years later and began eating young trees. Loggers cut larger trees. The forests were gone before French emperor Napoléon was exiled to the island after his final defeat in 1815.

Even a single predator can tip the delicate balance toward extinction. In 1894 a lighthouse keeper brought a cat with him to tiny Saint Stephen Island, just off the south island of New Zealand. Like many cats, this one went hunting, and brought its master many small birds, with short tails, light-colored breasts, and mottled brown backs. The lighthouse keeper preserved about a dozen of the peculiar birds, which he sent to English bird specialists, who said they were a new species. However no others were ever seen. That one cat had killed them all. (Scientists later found that the birds had lived on the mainland until rats that traveled with early human settlers had killed them; the island had been their last refuge.)

Larger populations are harder to kill, but people have done it. The guns of European settlers were deadly to some North American animals. Huge flocks of passenger pigeons flew over the eastern United States in the early 1800s. Hunters shot hundreds of thousands of the birds, never thinking that they would wipe them out by the end of the nineteenth century. Hunters did not have to kill every passenger pigeon, just reduce their numbers too low to survive. The American bison almost suffered the same fate. Millions roamed the great plains at the start of the 1800s, but only a few hundred were left at the end of the century.

A hundred years later, the great plains have no room for huge herds of bison. People have fenced the land. Much of it is farmed; most of the rest is pasture, set aside as grazing land for cattle.

Changing the World

The problem goes far beyond hunting. The occupation of this planet by more than five billion human beings has changed it in ways that are crowding out wildlife.

People began farming about 10,000 years ago. Farming probably started on open land, but later farmers cleared the forests of Europe. Native American farmers also cleared the land by burning brush and trees, but most of eastern North America was still forested when European settlers arrived in the 1600s. The Europeans cut down trees, and by 1800 farms covered most of New England. Farmers later moved west, clearing other forests that had better soil, and today trees again cover much of New England. They are young trees, however, and if you look closely you can see old rock walls that mark the borders of abandoned fields. Very little ancient forest is left in the United States today. Now tropical countries are clearing their forests, cutting trees for lumber and to open land for farming. Many scientists warn that clearing tropical rain forests could cause devasating extinctions.

No one recorded what was lost when people cleared the forests of North America and Europe. Explorers and settlers saw large animals, like wolves, bears, moose, beaver, and deer, fade back into the woods. They paid little attention to insects and small plants, so they would not have noticed if some went extinct. Most plants and animals leave few recognizable fossils, especially if the land is farmed. We may have missed many extinctions.

Scientists believe tropical rain forests hold far more species than temperate forests. They have explored only small areas, but they have found a great variety of plants and animals. Some insects live only in one type of tree in a small area. Clear a few square miles of tropical forest, and you could wipe them out. The problem is that people are clearing tropical forests today at a rate of 20,000 to 40,000 square miles (60,000 to 100,000 square kilometers) a year. That's about the area of South Carolina.

We are still finding new birds and mammals in the tropics. One example is a new species of bishop bird, found in early 1992 in Dar es Salaam, Tanzania. Four were discovered in a cage filled with many other captured birds, which were going to be shipped to the United States or Europe as pets. Two were found dead, however, and the other two died within two days. No one knows how many of the rare birds remain.

The Last Giants

The spread of people also endangers the last earthly giants: rhinos, elephants, and hippos. The rhinoceros is in the worst trouble. Living space for these animals is a problem; it takes 20 to 250 acres (8 to 100 hectares) to support one rhino. Poachers kill rhinos for their horns. And rhinos do not make good neighbors because they sometimes charge people.

Rhinos first evolved about 40 million years ago, and 100 to 300 species have lived since then. Like their cousins the horses, they began small and grew larger. A hornless rhino called Baluchitherium or Indrico-therium, which lived about 25 million years ago, was among the largest land mammals known. It weighed about 11 tons, had shoulders 18 feet (5.5 meters) high, and measured some 30 feet (9 meters) from the tip of its nose to its rear legs. Ice Age humans made cave paintings of the woolly rhinoceros, which vanished at the end of the Ice Age. Now only five species of rhino survive, and all are rare: 4,800 southern white rhinos, under 2,000 Great Indian rhinos, 3,600 black rhinos, 700 Sumatran rhinos, and a mere 60 Javan rhinos, making them the rarest large animal on the planet. The numbers have dropped as the human population has spread; in the late Middle Ages, hundreds of thousands of Indian rhinos lived in northern India, Pakistan, and the surrounding areas.

Climate Change

Many more species may be added to the endangered list if human actions continue to change global climate. We have seen that climate change is a suspect in most mass extinctions. We could even call the effects of an asteroid impact a type of climate change. Now people are changing climate in a different way, by putting into the air gases that trap heat and warm the surface of the planet. The most important are carbon dioxide and methane (sometimes called marsh gas). We call these greenhouse gases because they trap heat somewhat like the way a greenhouse does.

It is hard to measure how much we have changed the climate. Weather varies naturally, and accurate temperature records for most places go back only a little over 100 years. In the course of that time, average temperatures have risen about .9 degrees Fahrenheit, or .5 degrees Celsius, with the changes smaller near the equator and larger toward the poles. That is much smaller than daily variations, but it matters because it could shift climate belts toward the poles. The hot, dry summers of central Texas could shift into the midwestern grain belt. Frozen tundra might melt, and forests sprout in its place.

Some Russians like the idea of thawing Siberia, but warming could cause many problems elsewhere. Deserts and dry areas might spread. Plants might not be able to move as fast as the climate zones; they can migrate only by spreading seeds over a large area, and it takes time for trees to grow and spread more seeds. We may already be seeing the start of some problems. Coral reefs—victims of many earlier mass extinctions—are dying in some warm areas, perhaps because the water has grown too warm. Warming may have helped cause the droughts that have led to famines in Africa, although natural weather cycles and too much grazing on dry land may also be factors.

Pollution and acid rain also damage the environment. Pesticides like DDT almost caused the extinction of some birds of prey because they accumulate in the food chain. Each plant contains only a little pesticide, but it builds up in the bodies of the animals that eat the plants. Meat eaters, in turn, absorb the pesticide that had built up in plant eaters. Birds of prey are at the top of the food chain, so they accumulate the highest levels of the chemicals. The pesticide does not have to kill the birds to do damage. Too much DDT causes birds to lay eggs with thin, fragile shells, which are unlikely to hatch.

13

The Extinction Suspect List

Many scientists hoped that finding what killed the dinosaurs would solve the whole mystery of mass extinctions. At first chances looked good. Other great dyings seemed similar, with many species vanishing quickly, at least on a geologic time scale. Some studies seemed to show that the extinctions came regularly, about once every 26 to 30 million years. It was even thought that all extinctions might have had the same causes.

The picture no longer looks that simple. Excess iridium, shocked quartz, tektites, tsunami deposits, and the Chicxulub Crater all are solid evidence of at least one impact at the end of the Cretaceous. We are still not sure that the impact killed all of the dinosaurs or all of the other species that died at the same time. Even proving that an impact did kill the dinosaurs would not solve the mysteries of other mass extinctions. Different evidence was left at the scenes of the other great dyings. Impact fingerprints are missing. With our evidence in hand, we need to take another look at the suspect list.

The Impact Problem

Except for the end of the Cretaceous we have little solid evidence of large impacts at times of mass extinctions. The rocks hold a few hints of other possible matches. A few rocks from the time of the late Devonian extinctions contain tektites and excess iridium—but other rocks the same age do not. Scientists also have found excess iridium and tektites in rocks about 37 million years old, a time when some extinctions did happen—but not in all rocks that age. The iridium layers and tektites also may not match the dates of the extinctions. They may be from smaller impacts that caused local disasters—like the giant volcanic explosion described in chapter 11—but not global extinctions.

Another impact fingerprint, shocked quartz, also is rare. We saw in chapter 10 that scientists found some at the end of the Triassic in Europe, but the pattern is puzzling. The shocked quartz is in three separate layers. We don't know if it came from three impacts, or from debris from a single impact that washed into the sea at different times. Other rocks formed at the same time don't contain shocked quartz. Does that mean that the impacts were small? We don't know.

Nor do we know how much evidence time has destroyed, like fingerprints washed off a car door by rain. Tektites slowly turn to other minerals, so they are not likely to survive more than 100 million years. (Geologists were surprised to find them near the Devonian extinction of 367 million years ago.) Worms and other small animals that burrow in the ocean floor can spread excess iridium through other layers, smudging its fingerprints in the geologic record.

This lack of evidence makes it hard to blame impacts for all mass extinctions. Moreover, some big craters do not match any known extinction. Scientists very carefully dated the Manicouagan Crater in Quebec and the end of the Triassic. They didn't match. At 40 miles (70 kilometers) Manicouagan is a big crater, but it doesn't match the 110-mile (180-kilometer) Chicxulub Crater. Maybe it wasn't big enough, or maybe it takes a special type of impact to cause an extinction.

The type of impact may matter a lot. Was the object a solid rocky asteroid, or a dirty-snowball comet? How large was it? How fast was it moving? Did it hit the ground at an angle, or crash down from straight overhead? Did it hit land or sea? What kind of rocks did it hit? All these things may be important both in what evidence is left and in how the impact affects the earth.

Asteroids contain more iridium than comets, so an asteroid impact will yield more iridium—leaving a clearer fingerprint for geologists. The damage from an impact depends more on its mass and speed than on the nature of the object. A big comet impact could do as much damage as an asteroid, without leaving an iridium fingerprint. However, a comet would leave other impact fingerprints—shocked quartz and tektites.

Impact effects also depend on how an object hits the earth. Look for meteors at night, and you will see that they come from all directions at different speeds. So do big objects. We think that objects probably cause less damage if they hit the earth head-on than if they strike at a low angle, ripping a long way through the atmosphere. An object hitting at a low angle might make a series of craters, like ones recently found in Argentina. However we don't know much about the differences for large impacts.

As we saw when we talked about the Chicxulub Crater in chapter 8, the target also matters. An impact in sulfur-rich limestone may have caused far more damage than one in hard volcanic rock. Again, however, we don't know the details.

Volcanoes

We saw earlier that it is hard to blame volcanoes for the Cretaceous extinctions. The large eruptions in India may not have done the dinosaurs much good, but there is little evidence that they wiped them out, or caused other extinctions at the same time.

We saw in chapter 9, however, that there are some volcanic fingerprints at the end of the Permian. The huge eruptions that produced the Siberian Traps yielded 400,000 cubic miles (2 million cubic kilometers) of lava, making them the biggest in the geologic record. The eruptions came suspiciously close to the end of the Permian. Other eruptions that were not quite as large came close to other extinctions.

Yet the evidence is purely circumstantial. We don't know how huge volcanic eruptions might have caused extinctions, only that they came at about the same time. These eruptions poured liquid lava onto the planet's surface, but they were not explosions that blasted large amounts of sky-darkening dust high into the atmosphere. We don't know if the eruptions released enough gases to block sunlight, or alter climate in some other way. Volcanoes have to remain on the suspect list, but we can't point the finger too strongly.

Are Extinctions Periodic?

Not all the evidence of mass extinctions shows up in specific rocks. Scientists counting extinctions through the past few hundred million years found an interesting pattern on their charts. When they drew a graph of the number of extinctions at different times, they found peaks about every 26 to 30 million years. This sort of pattern always interests scientists because it may be a clue that the same thing caused different extinctions.

Could extinctions be periodic, happening at regular times? If so, what could cause them? Different theories have blamed impacts and volcanoes.

One idea is that the sun might have a faint companion star with an orbit that came near the sun once every 26 million years. When the faint star approached the sun, it would pull comets out of their orbits beyond Pluto. Some comets would go into the inner solar system, and a few would hit the earth, causing mass extinctions, and earning the companion star its name, Nemesis. No such star is known, but the last extinctions blamed on it were 10 to 15 million years ago, so it should be far away and hard to find. (It also would be no immediate threat, since it would not return for at least 10 million years.)

It's an interesting idea, which inspired a couple of books and at least one science fiction novel. Binary stars are common in our stellar neighborhood. But the Nemesis theory has serious problems. The companion star would come too close to other stars for its orbit to be stable. Astronomers have looked for it, but so far have found no trace of it.

Another theory blames hot rock rising from a layer close to the earth's metallic core. The theory says that streams of hot rock, like bubbles in water close to boiling, start moving upward fairly regularly—every 26 to 30 million years. When they reach the surface the hot rock causes massive eruptions of lava, like the Siberian Traps and the Indian deposits. This, too, is an interesting idea, but we don't know if it is true or how the eruptions could have caused extinctions.

In fact mass extinctions probably do not happen regularly. Scientists got the 26-million-year period by counting some fairly small peaks as mass extinctions. It is hard to find a dividing line between those smaller extinctions and the background of natural extinctions. So some of those peaks may not be real. Even if the peaks are real, the 26-million-year period may not be. Some scientists think it may be the sort of pattern sometimes seen in random numbers. Flip a coin often enough, and sooner or later it will come up heads five times in a row.

Environmental Change

Could changes in the environment have caused some mass extinctions? Climate and sea level did change at the times of some mass extinctions, making them likely suspects. We also worry about global climate change today. However some big questions remain.

Cooler ocean water may have wiped out early trilobites in the Cambrian and other sea animals at the end of the Ordovician, as we saw in chapter 11. Yet big changes have little effect at other times. Ice sheets have advanced and retreated many times in North America and Western Europe during the past 2 million years. The ice cooled the sea as well as the land. Yet no signs have been found of mass extinctions of shelly animals in the North Atlantic Ocean. Giant mammals did die out at the end of the last ice age, but people may have helped in their extinction.

Sea level can change quickly. It rose 300 feet (90 meters) in thousands of years as the great ice sheets on North America and Europe melted after the last ice age. The greatest drop in sea level in the geological record, over 660 feet (200 meters) came at the end of the Permian. That was the time of the worst mass extinction in the geologic record. The great dying hit animals fixed to the ocean floor much harder than those that could swim to deeper water. The shallow seas shrank as the oceans re-retreated, leaving only one-quarter as much ocean floor as there was earlier in the Permian. The link seems solid. Yet the rise and fall of sea level during the last two million years of ice ages did not wipe out ocean animals.

It is clear that climate change can cause extinctions. We can see it at work today, slowly killing plants and animals left from earlier times when the climate was different. Cypress trees still grow in isolated parts of the Sahara desert, relics of a wetter time a few thousand years ago. The old trees are still growing, but the desert now is too dry for new ones to sprout.

We can see the same thing in the southwestern United States, which grew hotter and dryer as the ice retreated. Once, forests covered much of Arizona, but the lowlands became deserts as the climate warmed. Forests retreated up the mountains, where it was cooler and wetter. They survive on the heights as "sky islands," isolated from one another by the deserts below, with climates similar to land far to the north. One sky island on the top of Mount Graham is home to a couple of hundred red squirrels that have evolved into a distinct subspecies after 10,000 years of isolation. Seventeen other plants and animals live on top of the mountain but nowhere else in the world. If the climate grows too much warmer or dryer, it could kill the forest and doom the plants and animals that live in it.

The problem with blaming environmental change for extinctions is that it doesn't answer why. Something must have changed the climate or sea level. That something was the real cause of the extinctions. Remember, an impact kills plants and animals not by landing on them, but by changing the environment so much that they cannot survive. What was it that made the environment change?

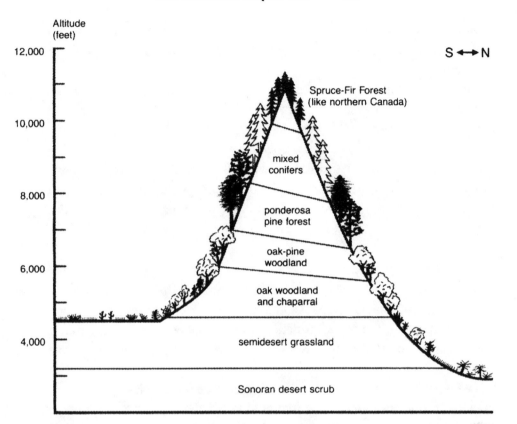

Altitude (feet)

S ←→ N

Spruce-Fir Forest
(like northern Canada)

mixed
conifers

ponderosa
pine forest

oak-pine
woodland

oak woodland
and chaparral

semidesert grassland

Sonoran desert scrub

Climate zones on Mount Graham in Arizona. Climbing up the mountain is the same as going farther north; the zones near the top are found in Canada. (Based on drawing from Coalition to Save Mount Graham)

That is a good question. Scientists are still trying to learn what causes ice ages and other changes in climate. Positions of the continents may be important; ice ages tend to occur when a continent is isolated at one pole. Ocean currents and the locations of mountain chains also influence climate. Small periodic changes in the earth's orbit may make ice sheets grow and retreat about every 100,000 years during our current ice age. Living things or reactions with rocks or the oceans may change levels of carbon dioxide, affecting climate through greenhouse warming. Some scientists think that the formation of thick layers of coal about 300 million years ago removed so much carbon dioxide from the air that the planet cooled enough to cause an ice age. But many questions remain about climate.

We know that sea level changes with the growth and melting of ice sheets, making it depend on climate. Other things can also change sea level, like the opening of ocean basins and the collisions of continents. No one knows where all the ocean water went at the end of the Permian period. Did ice sheets form somewhere? Did the land rise suddenly, then settle later—perhaps after the Siberian Traps started to erupt? Did cracks open up somewhere, creating a new ocean basin or a new place to put the water? Or did something else happen? We don't know.

Other Effects

Environmental change, impacts, and massive volcanic eruptions are only some suspects in the mass extinction mystery. Over the years, scientists have suggested many others. Some are clearly wrong, but others belong on the suspect list.

We saw in chapter 4 that evolution occurs because living things compete with one another. Those that best match the environment survive; those that don't, die. We normally think of evolution as moving slowly, but sometimes it can move fast. Suppose, for example, some creature made an evolutionary breakthrough, which let it spread in large numbers all over the world in 10,000 years. It might kill or crowd out other animals, making them extinct. Human beings have done just that. A few other animals like trilobites have spread rapidly in the past. But even fierce predators don't seem to have caused past mass extinctions.

Extinctions can occur when changes in sea level or continental collisions put together two groups of animals that evolved apart. That happened, as we saw, when the Panama land bridge opened a route between North and South America three million years ago. Many South American mammals lost the competition with mammals from North America and went extinct.

What about disease? It could wipe out individual species, but mass extinctions are very unlikely. The reason is that diseases are specialized; they affect no more than a few species, and often only one.

What about other disasters? Some giant stars explode in huge bursts of energy called supernovas. Supernovas are rare, but one might have exploded close enough to cause problems sometime in the earth's 4.5-billion-year history. If it did, the supernova would have left its own distinctive fingerprints, rare elements that form in supernova explosions. Scientists have looked for those fingerprints, but so far have not found them.

No Simple Answers

We like to solve mysteries with a simple answer that points to a single cause, like, "The asteroid did it." Life is not that simple. The network of life on our planet is complex and interwoven. It is both fragile and tough. Living things that can survive as drastic a change as the end of the Ice Age 18,000 years ago are vulnerable to fairly small amounts of a pesticide like DDT. Mass extinctions seem to tell us when the fabric of life broke down.

It may be that no single thing causes mass extinctions. Many things may have to happen together. Perhaps the dinosaurs died because they were vulnerable and the asteroid hit in a very bad place. The giant Ice Age mammals might have survived to the present if people had not come to North America when the animals were stressed by climate change.

The discovery of excess iridium at the end of the Cretaceous has led us on a fascinating trail. It got people thinking long and hard about the mystery of mass extinctions. By studying extinctions, we have learned a lot about evolution as well as extinctions. The story is not over. Most mysteries are not solved. Plenty of work remains for anyone curious about the course of life and evolution.

14

Looking Forward

In the earlier chapters we looked back at past extinctions. That can teach us about how life has evolved. It can also give us an idea of what the future might hold. Should we worry about asteroid impacts? Are there other potential catastrophes? Could we human beings be causing a new round of extinctions?

The Impact Danger

The Chicxulub Crater shows that big impacts can happen, with devastating effects. While hunting for that crater geologists found many smaller ones around the world, which apparently did not cause mass extinctions. It must take a big impact, and it may take one in a certain type of rock. Perhaps life can withstand an impact that makes a hole the size of a big city much better than one the size of Connecticut.

One way to assess impact danger is to count the objects in the solar system that might hit the earth. Asteroids in the main belt between Mars and Jupiter are a safe distance away. We have to look for objects that cross Earth's orbit. That includes comets and some asteroids—some of them probably dead comets that have stopped releasing the gases that give young comets their distinctive bright halos and tails. (Dead comets are almost black, darker than rocky asteroids.)

Small objects hit the earth very often. You can see tiny particles burning in the upper atmosphere as meteors streaking across the sky on a dark night. The rare bright meteors, called fireballs, are larger pebbles, which also burn up in the air. Only a few objects are large and solid enough to pass all the way through the air and land on the surface as meteorites. Those meteorites, and rocks brought back from the moon by Apollo astronauts, are our only samples of material from space.

All we see of meteors is the bright tail they make as they hit the atmosphere. Small meteors are too faint to see in space, and even larger objects are very hard to observe, because they shine only by reflecting sunlight. The farther they are from Earth, the fainter they appear. Even an asteroid a couple of miles (about three kilometers) across is too faint to detect during most of its orbit. It is visible only when it comes close, but then it is moving very fast. It's like watching cars from the side of a highway—you can't see much when they're far away, and they move too fast when they're close.

Most astronomers pay little attention to asteroids. Some have called these chunks of rock and ice "vermin of the sky" because they can get in the way of other objects that the scientists think more interesting. The few astronomers interested in asteroids have been searching for objects that might hit the earth since people began worrying about impacts. They look for objects that move across the sky at the right speed to be asteroids or comets. They measure their positions carefully and use that information to calculate their orbits around the sun.

So far scientists have found well over a hundred objects that approach the earth. The smallest, only 30 feet (9 meters) across, was detected only because it happened to pass nearby when a telescope was pointed in the right direction. Most are between .3 and 1.3 miles (.5 to 2 kilometers) across, but a couple come close to the 6-mile (10-kilometer) size that hit the planet 65 million years ago. One is Comet Swift-Tuttle, which was rediscovered in late 1992 after being lost for over a century. It briefly made headlines when rough calculations of its orbit showed it

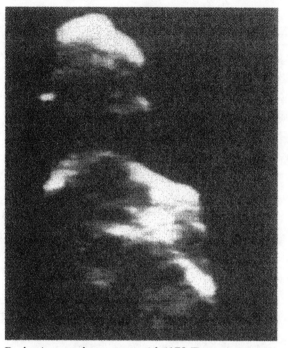

Radar image shows asteroid 4179 Toutatis is a pair of objects 2.5 and 1.5 miles (4 and 2.5 kilometers) across. (Courtesy of Jet Propulsion Laboratory)

had a slight chance of colliding with the earth in 2126, but later observations showed it would miss by 25 million miles (40 million kilometers). No known objects are on a collision course with the planet.

The known objects are only a small fraction of the total. Gene Shoemaker estimates that over a thousand objects larger than .6 mile (1 kilometer) approach the earth. Because the larger objects are brighter, astronomers are more likely to have found them than the smaller ones, if they have small orbits and circle the sun every few years. That means there is a good chance that the largest near-Earth asteroid known, 5-mile (8-kilometer) 1627 Ivar, is the largest one that exists. However, large comets are easier to miss because their orbits take them so far from the sun that they become too faint to detect. That is how Comet

Swift-Tuttle got lost, although it is probably about the same size as Ivar.

It is good news that nothing as big as the object that formed the Chicxulub Crater comes near the earth. However, a smaller impact could still cause big problems, and there probably are thousands of unknown objects larger than .3 mile (.5 kilometer) which could hit the planet with little or no warning. An impact too small to cause mass extinctions could devastate the planet. A species can still survive even if 90 percent of the individuals die. Human civilization might not.

In the summer of 1991 I went to a meeting in San Juan Capistrano, California, where scientists talked about the dangers of asteroid impact. They worried about how big an impact it would take to destroy human civilization. The impact need not kill everybody right away. It need only make crops fail for a time long enough to exhaust global food reserves. The high-yield crops in developed countries might be more vulnerable than traditional crops, which can tolerate harsher conditions.

How big an impact would that take? The scientists guessed it would take an object of .3 to 3 miles (.5 to 5 kilometers). How likely are such impacts? The guesses ranged from once every 100,000 years to once every 10 million. However, the scientists were not very sure of their numbers. We know little about the number of objects that might hit the earth or how impacts would affect civilization.

Some scientists thought small impacts were a more likely danger than big ones. In 1908 a 100-foot (30-meter) chunk of ice or rock exploded in the atmosphere, leveling 800 square miles (2,000 square kilometers) of forest in the Tunguska region of Siberia. We were lucky that time. Nobody was hurt because nobody lived there. The same explosion would have been an incredible disaster over a major city like New York, London, Tokyo, or Mexico City. It would be a disaster in a farm area. John Pike of the Federation of American Scientists estimated that a Tunguska event in a farming area of the midwest could kill 68,000 people and cause $4.5 billion in property damage.

We don't know how common Tunguska-type events are because they leave no crater on land and no trace in the ocean. The Tunguska blast was recorded, and it's doubtful anything else like it has happened in the

The devastation 4 miles (7 kilometers) from the center of the Tunguska explosion was still visible twenty years later, when the first Russian scientists arrived. (Courtesy of *Tass,* from Sovfoto)

last one hundred years, but a similar explosion could have gone unnoticed over the Pacific Ocean in 1700 or over much of the planet a couple of hundred years earlier.

The first step in assessing the asteroid danger is to look for objects that approach the earth. That can be done from the ground with small telescopes. Then astronomers can calculate the objects' orbits to see if any might hit the earth in the near future. If we knew in advance that an object did threaten the planet we might be able to deflect it. Large objects are not likely to threaten the earth in the near future, however; reckless automobile drivers are a far bigger risk to our individual survival than stray asteroids or comets.

Environmental Threats

The worst threat of future extinctions comes not from the sky but from ourselves. Humans have already changed the environment of our planet and caused many extinctions, as we saw in chapter 12. If current trends continue, the picture will only get worse.

More than five billion people already crowd the world. Experts predict that the number will pass ten billion in a century. Those additional people will need more room to live and to grow food. Perhaps we will learn to grow food more efficiently, but the extra people will still take more space from nature. That means less room for plants and animals to live. It means that more tropical forests will be cut to make room in

World Population—Millions

Human population has risen steadily from about 300 million in ancient Roman times to about 5 billion today and is expected to pass 10 billion in the next century. (Data from World Resources Institute)

the developing countries where population is growing fastest. It means that deserts may spread more as people try to raise crops or animals on land that is too dry for farming.

The tropical forests are very rich in species, and as they shrink, so will the number of species. We may never see most of them. Scientists have cataloged 1.4 million species of living things, and estimate that 10 to 100 million species live on Earth today. We have found the largest and most obvious ones and the ones that live where most scientists are. It is easy to miss species that live in small areas. Scientists found the unusual animals on Mount Graham in Arizona only because astronomers had chosen the site for an observatory. Some people worry that the observatory may take land that the endangered squirrels need, but in a way the squirrels were lucky. No one would have done anything to protect them if the astronomers had not picked that mountain. Few places in the tropics have been studied as carefully as the top of Mount Graham.

Large animals have different problems. We know they exist, but we have little room for them to live. Poor people will kill them for food or to profit by selling elephant ivory or rhinoceros horn. Poaching is such a big problem that conservationists have even cut the horns off living rhinos to save the animals from hunters who want the horns.

Other problems affect the whole planet. People are adding carbon dioxide and methane to the atmosphere. These greenhouse gases trap heat and make the earth warmer. Warmer climate threatens species from tropical corals to the red squirrels of Mount Graham. Pollution and acid rain are further problems that threaten other species.

The movement of plants and animals around the world is another threat. Imported competitors can wipe out native species, as North American mammals wiped out the natives of South America. Islands have fared the worst at human hands. People and the animals they brought with them have killed many species on islands from Madagascar to New Zealand. Imported plants and animals like the gypsy moth and zebra mussel are causing problems today. The Nile perch has eaten up many unique species of small fish native to Lake Victoria in Africa. Rabbits are a problem in Australia. The list could go on and on.

We are making some progress. We are trying to control some pollution. The nations of the world agreed to stop using chlorinated fluorocarbons (CFCs), because those gases destroy ozone high in the atmosphere, which blocks harsh ultraviolet rays from the sun. Many countries are trying to slow or stop the cutting of forests. But there is much to do, and it is not clear how successful we will be.

We cannot stop extinctions completely any more than we can stop time. Extinction is a part of the evolution of life; the planet itself is always changing. Old species must go extinct just as new ones must evolve, but human beings are causing extinctions at one thousand to ten thousand times the natural rate—the greatest wave of extinctions since the end of the Cretaceous 65 million years ago. The clearing of tropical forests, the increase in population, and other human activity could wipe out over one quarter of the species on the planet in the next fifty years, warns a report from the National Academy of Sciences.

Such large extinctions could devastate the environment. Forests moderate tropical climate; deserts may spread if the forests are destroyed. Species depend on one another in ways we often do not understand, so the loss of one may lead to other extinctions, like the death of the dodo almost led to the extinction of a tree on Mauritius. Scientists do not understand why some songbird populations vary, and what sort of winter environments they need in tropical forests. We know of no other species that has caused more devastation than humans, but we can decide to stop.

A View from the Far Future

Suppose we could jump 65 million years into the future and become paleontologists in a world that had forgotten about people. What signs would we find of the extinctions that humans have already caused?

We would find that most large land animals disappeared rather suddenly. It would be hard to prove if they died in a few years or ten thousand years. We might note that some animals seemed to vanish a little earlier than others, with the woolly mammoths, mastodons, and giant ground sloths dying out before the dodos and moas. But we might blame that on the imperfect fossil record. We would see the bison population of the American West drop suddenly, but we wouldn't find fossils of the domestic cattle that replaced them. (The meat industry does not leave bones around to become fossils.) If elephants and rhinos are lucky and survive the next few hundred years, we might find their fossils after the extinction layer, and wonder how they managed to escape.

We might also see the sudden spread of a large ape that had left few fossils before the extinctions. These large apes would seem to have arrived about the time of the extinctions. A few other animals—dogs and cats, rats and mice—would seem to have spread with the large apes. We would wonder what made those animals suddenly so successful.

We would find few extinctions of shelly ocean animals at the same time, unless we took our samples from some badly polluted harbor, or unless human beings do severe harm to the ocean in the future.

If we didn't know what had happened, we might spend a long time wondering about the mystery of those human-caused extinctions.

Glossary

AMMONOID   an extinct marine animal related to the octopus and squid, with a spiral shell that had elaborate patterns inside.

ANHYDRITE   sedimentary rock rich in calcium sulfate; it releases sulfuric acid into the air if vaporized.

ASTEROID   a rocky body smaller than a planet that orbits the sun; most are between Mars and Jupiter, but some approach the earth.

BOUNDARY LAYER   the layer that divides rocks formed during two successive periods. The best known is the K-T boundary layer, which marks the end of the Cretaceous (K) period and the start of the Tertiary (T) period 65 million years ago.

COMET   an object orbiting the sun that releases a bright cloud of gas as it approaches the sun; it contains ice as well as rock and dust.

CRUST   the solid layer of the earth.

DARWINIAN EVOLUTION   a theory that living things evolve gradually most of the time, in contrast to punctuated equilibrium, a theory that living things evolve in spurts.

EVOLUTION   changes in living things that make the descendants differ from their ancestors.

EXTINCTION   death of all individuals in a group of plants or animals, so none are left alive.

FOSSIL   remains or traces of a plant or animal preserved in rock; dinosaur bones and footprints are both fossils.

GONDWANA   the "supercontinent" made up of Africa, South America, Antarctica, India, and Australia, which existed from about 500 to 150 million years ago.

GREENHOUSE EFFECT   the trapping of heat energy by gases in the lower atmosphere, preventing energy from escaping and warming the earth.

ICE AGE   a time when large polar areas are covered by thick ice sheets and the earth is unusually cool.

IGNEOUS   rocks formed from molten rock.

INTERGLACIAL   a break during an ice age when glaciers melt back but do not vanish completely. We live in an interglacial period.

IRIDIUM   a heavy metal that is very rare on the earth's surface but more common in asteroids. Excess iridium is a sign of asteroid impact.

LIMESTONE   sedimentary rock formed mostly of calcium carbonate from the shells of marine animals; releases carbon dioxide if vaporized.

MAGMA   molten rock.

MANTLE   the thick layer of soft or molten rock between the crust and the metallic core of the earth.

MASS EXTINCTION   the extinction of many species at about the same time.

MEGAFAUNA   giant animals, usually meaning those that lived in the last ice age.

METAMORPHIC   rocks altered by heat and/or pressure when they were buried deep underground.

METEOR   strictly speaking, the flash of light seen when an object from space burns up in the earth's atmosphere. The object itself often is called a meteor, but the proper word is meteoroid.

METEORITE   a piece of space debris found on the earth's surface.

NAUTILOID   a marine animal related to the octupus and squid, with conical or spiral shell. Related to the extinct ammonoids.

PANGAEA   the "world continent" formed when most of the continents came together between about 300 and 170 million years ago.

PLATE TECTONICS   the motion of rigid plates about the surface of the earth, changing positions of the continents.

PLUTONIC   rocks that formed from liquid rock that never reached the surface before becoming solid.

PUNCTUATED EQUILIBRIUM   the theory that living things remain in stable states most of the time but evolve rapidly as they change between stable forms.

RADIOACTIVE   an atomic nucleus that breaks apart on its own because it is unstable, releasing energy.

SEDIMENT   a mass of small particles that collects somewhere, often at the bottom of water. Sedimentary rocks are formed from sediment.

SHOCKED QUARTZ   quartz crystals containing tiny flaws caused by an explosion; impacts produce more shock flaws than other explosions.

STRATIGRAPHY   the science of deducing the age and origins of rocks from the way layers are formed.

TEKTITE   glassy rock formed when molten rock was splattered into the air by an impact.

TRILOBITE   an extinct marine animal with three distinct "lobes" running the length of its body; the first abundant fossils.

VOLCANIC   rocks that formed from liquid rock at or near the surface of the earth.

Further Reading

Few of these books are written for young readers. However, none requires special knowledge of science, and all contain much fascinating information about geology and evolution.

Elsom, Derek. *Earth*. New York: Macmillan, 1992. Overview of geology; well illustrated.

Erickson, Jon. *An Introduction to Fossils & Minerals*. New York and Oxford: Facts on File, 1992. Mostly about rocks.

. *Plate Tectonics: Unraveling the Mysteries of the Earth*. New York and Oxford: Facts on File, 1992. How the continents move and change.

Fenton, Carroll Lane, Mildred Adams Fenton, Patricia Vickers Rich, and Thomas Hewitt Rich. *The Fossil Book*. New York: Doubleday, 1989. Fossils and the evolution of life; well illustrated.

Lewin, Roger. *Thread of Life*. Washington, D.C.: Smithsonian Books, 1982. Evolution; well illustrated.

Marshall, Kim. *The Story of Life: From the Big Bang to You*. New York: Holt, Rinehart, & Winston, 1980. Evolution.

Pielou, E. C. *After the Ice Age: The Return of Life to Glaciated North America*. Chicago: University of Chicago Press, 1991. Changes that followed the end of the last ice age.

Raymo, Chet. *Biography of a Planet: Geology, Astronomy, and the Evolution of Life on Earth*. Englewood Cliffs, N.J.: Prentice-Hall, 1984.

Stanley, Steven M. *Extinction*. New York: Scientific American Books, 1987.

———. *The New Evolutionary Timetable*. New York: Basic Books, 1981.

Time-Life Books, *Evolution of Life*. Alexandria, Va.: Time-Life Books, 1992. Well illustrated.

———. *Planet Earth*. Alexandria, Va.: Time-Life Books, 1992. Well illustrated.

Weiner, Jonathan. *Planet Earth*. New York: Bantam, 1986.

Index

Page references in italics indicate material in tables.

Printed in the United States
By Bookmasters